IMITATION

Imitation: The Basics is an engaging introduction to the topic of imitation behavior in humans, providing a summary of existing scientific research on imitation, covering everything from examples of imitation across each developmental stage to animal imitation such as monkeys imitating each other.

The authors argue that imitation forms the foundation of long-lasting relationships, including those between children and parents, as well as intimate partners. Structured to resemble a human lifetime, chapters explore the reasons behind why people imitate, and address imitation across all phases of life, starting from infancy, childhood, adolescence, adulthood and ending with late adulthood. The authors describe characteristic forms of imitation that occur in these life stages and provide answers to the following important questions: Who do humans imitate? Who is more likely to imitate others? What kind of behaviors do humans imitate? Is there a dark side of imitation? When do humans imitate each other? And are there cultural differences in imitation?

Written in a clear and accessible style, this book is perfect for undergraduate students of social psychology, developmental psychology and neuroscience, as well as professionals, academics and any general readers interested in research about human social behavior.

Naomi van Bergen, MSc., is a PhD student at the Behavioural Science Institute at the University of Nijmegen, the Netherlands.

Allard R. Feddes, PhD, is an Assistant Professor at the Department of Social Psychology at the University of Amsterdam, the Netherlands.

Liesbeth Mann, PhD, is a University Lecturer at the Department of Social Psychology at the University of Amsterdam, the Netherlands.

Bertjan Doosje, PhD, is an Associate Professor at the Department of Social Psychology at the University of Amsterdam, the Netherlands.

The Basics Series

The Basics is a highly successful series of accessible guidebooks which provide an overview of the fundamental principles of a subject area in a jargon-free and undaunting format.

Intended for students approaching a subject for the first time, the books both introduce the essentials of a subject and provide an ideal springboard for further study. With over 50 titles spanning subjects from artificial intelligence (AI) to women's studies, *The Basics* are an ideal starting point for students seeking to understand a subject area.

Each text comes with recommendations for further study and gradually introduces the complexities and nuances within a subject.

EDUCATIONAL NEUROSCIENCE
CATHY ROGERS AND MICHAEL S. C. THOMAS

CLASSICAL MYTHOLOGY (SECOND EDITION)
RICHARD MARTIN

PLAY DIRECTING: THE BASICS
DAMON KIELY

ARCHAEOLOGICAL THEORY
ROBERT CHAPMAN

INFORMATION SCIENCE
JUDITH PINTAR AND DAVID HOPPING

DEATH AND RELIGION
CANDI K. CANN

DIGITAL RELIGION
HEIDI A. CAMPBELL AND WENDI BELLAR

DRAMATURGY
ANNE M. HAMILTON AND WALTER BYONGSOK CHON

HINDUISM
NEELIMA SHUKLA-BHATT

RELIGION IN AMERICA 2E
MICHAEL PASQUIER

FINANCE (FOURTH EDITION)
ERIK BANKS

IMITATION: THE BASICS
NAOMI VAN BERGEN, ALLARD R. FEDDES, LIESBETH MANN AND BERTJAN DOOSJE

For a full list of titles in this series, please visit www.routledge.com/The-Basics/book-series/B

IMITATION

THE BASICS

Naomi van Bergen, Allard R. Feddes,
Liesbeth Mann and Bertjan Doosje

LONDON AND NEW YORK

Designed cover image: © Getty Images

First published 2023
by Routledge
4 Park Square, Milton Park, Abingdon, Oxon OX14 4RN

and by Routledge
605 Third Avenue, New York, NY 10158

Routledge is an imprint of the Taylor & Francis Group, an informa business

British Library Cataloguing-in-Publication Data
A catalogue record for this book is available from the British Library

ISBN: 978-1-032-00660-4 (hbk)
ISBN: 978-1-032-00542-3 (pbk)
ISBN: 978-1-003-17505-6 (ebk)

DOI: 10.4324/9781003175056

Typeset in Bembo
by codeMantra

CONTENTS

ACKNOWLEDGMENTS

We imitate each other a lot! Why do we do this? Are some of us more likely to imitate than others? Does this depend on your age? Do animals imitate? And if so, what can we learn from that? And is there a dark side to imitation?

In this book, we summarize the state-of-the art knowledge about imitation. We answer the following two fundamental questions: (1) Why do humans imitate each other? and (2) How does imitation develop from infancy to late adulthood?

We like to express our gratitude to the following people at Routledge: Eleanor Taylor, Tori Sharpe, and Alex Howard. We would also like to thank the people of the "Exactitudes" project (exactitudes.com), who allowed us to use one of their photos for free. We can very much recommend you to take a look at this wonderful project that illustrates nicely how we imitate each other, perhaps sometimes without realizing it!

We have enjoyed writing this book. We hope you will enjoy reading this book! We hope it will open your eyes to how we (including yourself!) imitate each other in our daily lives. Usually for better, sometimes for worse...

The authors,
November 2022

THE ROOTS AND ROUTES OF IMITATION

INTRODUCTION

"Wah". A soft cry from a newborn baby in the middle of the night in a quiet and dark hospital room filled with 20 newborn babies. After a short silence, a second newborn baby starts to cry as well. "Wah wah". Within seconds, a third baby joins in. Within one minute after the first soft cry, all the newborn babies in the room are crying loud and clearly. What has happened here? Is this imitation or what?

Imitation is a powerful human tendency. We imitate each other a lot. Sometimes on purpose, such as when we imitate ideas of influencers or the way famous pop stars dress. And sometimes we are not so much aware of our tendency to imitate. For example, when we talk together, we tend to imitate each other's bodily posture without much awareness. Did the newborn babies in the hospital imitate intentionally? Or did they merely respond to one of the most upsetting sounds to humans (a crying baby)?

In this book, we answer fascinating questions about imitation: Why do we imitate? Which behaviors do we imitate? When do we imitate (in which situations)? Who do we imitate? Who is more likely to imitate? How is imitation related to the brain? Is there a dark side to imitation? Do other animals also imitate? And are there cultural differences in imitation?

WHY IS IMITATION IMPORTANT?

Imitation is important to humans. We learn by imitation. We have teachers, coaches, trainers, parents, caregivers, etc. They are all

DOI: 10.4324/9781003175056-1

likely to teach us how to do certain things by demonstrating to us how to do it. As such, imitation is a powerful learning tool. The teacher, coach, trainer, or parent performs certain behavior, and we (aim to) copy it as good as we can. This example behavior can range from relatively simple instructions (Parent: "A cat says 'meow'. Can you say 'meow'?" Child: "Meeeooow") to a relatively complex set of instructions (e.g., directors may first play a scene themselves in order to show actors how they should act in that scene). We assume the importance of imitation when we say that we have "to set a good example" (as a parent, as a boss, etc.). We know that people often follow examples. How do we know this?

Well, this is apparent from watching trends, fashions or styles. For example, in the way we dress, make music, dance, make art, use language, cook, and eat we follow trends, fashions and styles. Typically, these trends are "in fashion" for a certain time and then disappear (or we transform them). For example, the way we dress now is different from ten years ago as fashion has changed. Similarly, the things we eat today are different from ten years ago: in some parts of the world, we now eat less meat than ten years ago, for example. This list of trends in human behavior is endless.

These trends tell us two things: first, they indicate that we really do imitate, but, second, oftentimes only for a limited period of time. Thus, trends show us that there *is* a limit to our imitation. At one point, some of us no longer follow the general trend and want to take a different route. People start thinking "out of the box" and that is when new discoveries are made. And oftentimes we start new trends and start all over again with imitation!

THE ROOTS OF IMITATION

We humans have always lived in groups. First in hunter-gathering groups, later in agricultural groups, later again in industrialized cities, and nowadays we even live together digitally online! In all of these groups, people have imitated each other. This was an important way to learn about the (sometimes dangerous) world. How to make tools to hunt, where to find fruit and how to make fire to prepare food and scare predators – these were significant behaviors that have shaped the history of our world. These behaviors were transmitted via imitation. Children learned them via imitating their parents or other older people. Thus, imitation serves an *evolutionary function* (see also Chapter 2): without imitation, humans would not have been as successful as we are today. Following an evolutionary argument: we may have become relatively prone to imitate, because it has been such an effective way to adjust to changing environments. For example, when a new ice age started, humans were able to effectively deal with the challenges (i.e., using hides to dress warm). Therefore, it is possible that the people who frequently imitated were more likely to pass on their genes to the next generation. Over thousands of years, this created an ever more likely inclination in humans to imitate each other.

Interestingly, lots of other animals have survived due to imitation. This is most evident when we look at dangerous situations. When in danger, fear spreads quickly among animals. This is a useful strategy if you want to live a long life as illustrated in Figure 1.1!

Figure 1.1 Fear can lead to imitation in a lot of animals. In this case, seagulls fly away after one of them showed fear for the approaching dog. The seagull that is stubborn and does not fly away is less likely to survive. Consequently, such "stubborn" genes are not passed on to next generations as a result. In this way, evolution has shaped our imitation behavior.

Source: shutterstock.com.

BOX 1.1 ARE WE ALL UNIQUE INDIVIDUALS?

Not a question really: yes, of course, we are all unique individuals. There is no one on the whole planet that is like me. Yes, technically speaking, we share 50% of our genes with our parents, but we are so

Figure 1.2 These are pictures of 12 girls who (either knowingly or unknowingly) imitate others like them. *Exactitudes by Ari Versluis & Ellie Uyttenbroek.*

Source: exactitudes.com.

different from them, aren't we? We are all unique individuals! At least that is what we like to think...

Please have a look at the fantastic and self-confronting ongoing project "Exactitudes" (by photographer Ari Versluis and profiler Ellie Uyttenbroek) on this website: https://exactitudes.com/collectie/. Have a good look around at the website. On the website, you can find hundreds of series of 12 portraits of individuals, who imitate each other (perhaps without knowing or intention): They are look-alikes. See the pictures on the website for plenty of examples. In Figure 1.2, we give an example.

Now the important question: Can you find yourself on the website? Do you belong to one of the series? Could you potentially be one of the 12 portraits in a series? And then answer again this question: Are we all unique individuals? See also Chapter 2 on how we would like to balance our need to be unique individuals with our need to belong to groups.

THE TWO ROUTES OF IMITATION

Closely linked to the roots of imitation, we suggest that there are two routes to imitation (see also Chapter 2). The first route is the *learning* route. This route explains *how* we learn new behaviors by looking at others. We depict this route in Figure 1.3. It involves five steps. In Step 1, we are faced with an unfamiliar situation or problem. We wonder how we should solve this problem. In Step 2, we search for role models. Do other people have a clue on how to deal with this situation or problem that I face? If we see a useful role model, we imitate (Step 3). In Step 4, we can find out that it works. Finally, in Step 5, we are proud of ourselves, which results in high personal well-being. This will lead to sustainable behavior: we'll do it again like this next time around.

The second route to imitation is the *social* route and it is depicted in Figure 1.4. This route deals with social situations. When facing an unfamiliar social situation, we often wonder how we should behave (Step 1): What is appropriate in this situation? Again, when uncertain, people often search for role models (Step 2): What do others do? If we find a suitable role model, we start imitating the model (Step 3). Consequently, we may experience that other people start liking us, as

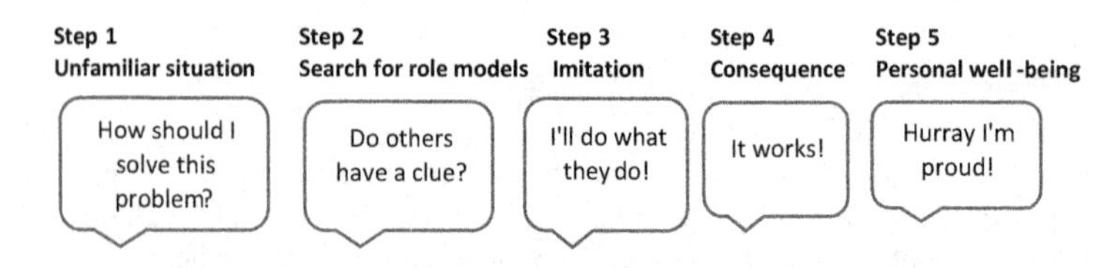

Figure 1.3 The *learning* route to imitation: five steps.

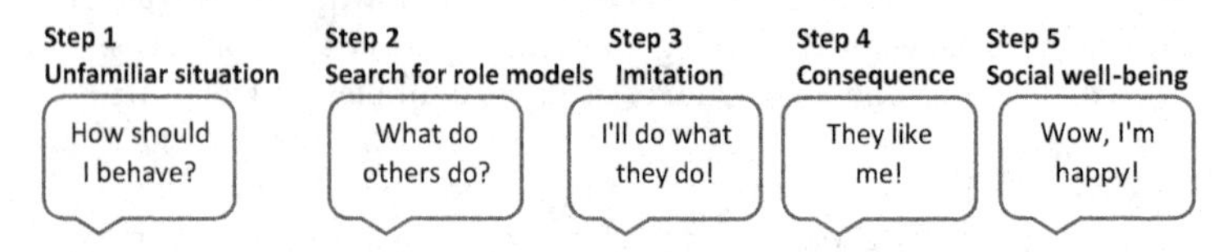

Figure 1.4 The *social* route to imitation: five steps.

people tend to like people who are similar to themselves (Step 4). This then may result in high social well-being (Step 5): Wow, I'm happy and I am glad to be part of this group! Subsequently, we will repeat this imitative behavior next time when we are in such a situation.

Both routes are similar in the sense that we search for role models when we feel *uncertain*. But they are different in that sometimes we actively search for *specific role models* to solve a difficult problem (the learning route), whereas in other times we aim to know how to behave socially in a situation by looking at how most others behave (the social route). They also have different endpoints: we can feel good about *ourselves* when we have solved a problem by imitating another person (the learning route), but we can feel good *as a group member* when we experience that other people like us after we have imitated them (the social route). When taking the social route, imitation can be seen as a social glue![1] You can actually take advantage of this fact, see Box 1.2 which explains how you can use imitation in order to become a millionaire…

BOX 1.2 HOW TO BECOME A MILLIONAIRE – A GOOD TIP FOR WAITERS/WAITRESSES!

Yes, of course, robbing a bank is the quickest route to becoming a millionaire. But if you do not have what it takes to rob a bank, please consider this option: become a waiter/waitress and follow this instruction carefully: literally imitate the orders that you receive! Come again? How does that work?

A fascinating study by psychologists has shown that when waiters exactly repeat an order using the customer's words, they receive a higher tip.[2] For example, consider the following conversation:

CUSTOMER: Can I have a cappuccino and a carrot cake, please?

WAITER: Yes, of course, so you want a cappuccino and a carrot cake.

In this case, the waiter repeats the order in the same words. But the conversation could easily have been as follows:

CUSTOMER: Can I have a cappuccino and a carrot cake, please?

WAITER: Yes, of course, I'll get it right away for you.

In both cases, one could argue, the waiter makes a favorable impression. But in situation 1, the waiter is bound to receive a higher tip than in situation 2. Why? Imitation!

The scientists do not exactly know why imitation works for the waiter. But we do know that when people imitate us, we tend to like them, most likely because we like ourselves. As a side note: this makes it less likely for people with depressive symptoms to follow the cycle from being imitated to feeling liked.

So, if we're embarking on a waiter/waitress career, we should make sure that we imitate the exact orders of our customers as closely as possible. This will result in lots of tips. And sure enough, one day, we'll be millionaires!

In Figures 1.3 and 1.4, we have sketched an ideal outcome: we imitate another person, and the problem is solved which makes us feel good about ourselves (Figure 1.3). Or other group members start liking me better, which makes me feel good because I feel accepted (Figure 1.4). However, unfortunately, life is not always that easy. Sometimes it does not work that way. For example, sometimes, imitating the wrong people might lead to negative outcomes for us, such as an incorrect answer to a problem, or others start to dislike us because we imitate them (although, as we shall see, that latter outcome is less likely to occur). When that happens, we may change our strategy. We can go back to Step 2 in both routes: We search for other potentially successful role models and start imitating them in hopes of a better outcome.

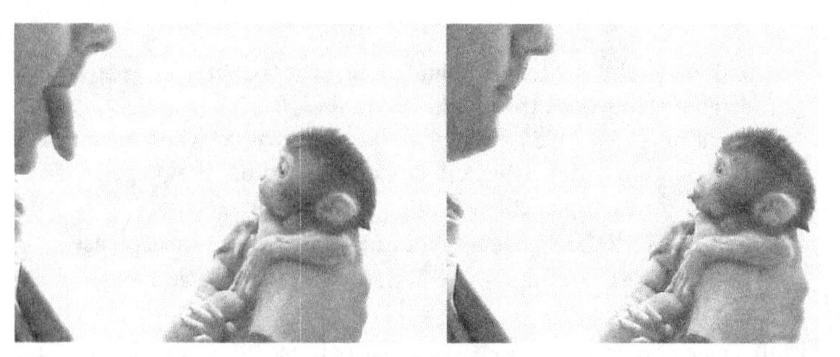

Figure 1.5 Monkey see, monkey do. Did you know that rhesus macaques as young as seven days old can mimic facial expressions of humans?[5]

Source: Gross, L. (2006). Evolution of neonatal imitation. *PLoS Biology, 4*(9), e311. https://doi.org/10.1371/journal.pbio.0040311. https://creativecommons.org/licenses/by/2.5/legalcode.

It is possible to distinguish two types of imitation: one is the imitation of simple gestures such as hand movements to move puzzle pieces (sometimes referred to as "mimicry" or the chameleon effect).[3,4] The other type involves copying of goal-directed behavior, such as putting the puzzle pieces together.

It makes sense to look at these two different types of imitation because, for example, young children are able to mimic simple hand movements but cannot imitate more complex goal-directed behavior (see Chapter 3). Similarly, when we get older, say above 70 years, we might be able to still mimic a simple hand movement. However, the capacity to imitate more complex movements with two hands will deteriorate by that age, unfortunately (see Chapter 7). We still might be able to stick out our tongue though, like the seven-day-old monkey in Figure 1.5.

OUTLINE OF THIS BOOK

Why do humans imitate others? In Chapter 2, existing social psychological and developmental psychological theories on imitation will be described. This includes an evolutionary perspective asserting that imitation is an adaptive form of learning (the *learning route*, see Figure 1.3) and a social psychology perspective claiming that imitation is associated with being liked by other group members (the *social route*, see Figure 1.4). In Chapter 2, we also discuss developmental psychological perspectives including theories of language acquisition and neurocognitive perspectives describing mirror neurons: where does imitation take place in the brain?

How does imitation behavior develop throughout our lives? In this book, we describe five developmental stages in life: infancy (Chapter 3), childhood (Chapter 4), adolescence (Chapter 5), adulthood (Chapter 6) and late adulthood (Chapter 7). We describe characteristic forms of imitation that occur in these life stages. In doing so, we provide answers to the following questions:

a. Who do humans imitate? Here, we describe studies on models who are more likely to be copied than others. For example, we describe the phenomenon that people are more likely to imitate celebrities (in arts, sports, etc.) in comparison with unknown people. This is called the *prestige bias*.
b. Who is more likely to imitate others? Here, we focus on who is more prone to imitate others. For example, adolescents are particularly prone to imitate their peers compared to people in other age groups. We will also focus on clinical disorders. For example, by focusing on disorders associated with *reduced* tendencies to imitation such as autism.
c. What *kind* of behaviors do humans imitate? Imitation can involve positive or negative behaviors. Take, for example, the "ice bucket challenge" where people across the world copied each other to raise money for charity. Other behavior that often involves imitation is demonstrating and collective action. Think of the "Black Lives Matter" movements. However, we will also focus on the so-called dark side of imitation, as described below (d).
d. Is there a dark side to imitation? Here, we focus on imitational behaviors with negative consequences. For example, in Chapter 5 on imitation in adolescence, we will describe the phenomenon of copycat suicide and give other examples when the human tendency to imitate is used questionably (e.g., the decision to join a criminal group or even a terrorist group).
e. When do humans imitate each other? Here, we focus on the role of the environment (do particular situations lead to more or less imitation), as well as on group processes (the influence other people have on the likelihood to imitate or not). For

example, when we feel uncertain, we are more likely to imitate behaviors of others in an attempt to reduce this uncertainty (see Step 1 in Figures 1.3 and 1.4). In line with this idea, at the beginning of COVID-19, people started buying toilet paper *en masse* (see Chapter 6 on imitation in adulthood). We also discuss the role of two types of social norms. *Descriptive* norms refer to people considering what others do. *Injunctive* social norms refer to the phenomenon that people's behavior that is "not normative" for the social group results in corrections (i.e., punishment) by other group members.

f. Are there cultural differences in imitation? Here, we focus on intercultural studies of imitation and the value people attach to it. For instance, imitation is seen as a form of flattery in some cultures, whilst in other cultures it is more likely to be seen as a form of unoriginality.

g. Do animals imitate? Here, we focus on imitation in the animal kingdom, including herd behaviors. We also pay attention to imitation between different species, such as monkeys imitating each other. We draw analogies between human imitation and animal imitation. For example, is the contagion of fear in humans similar to the behavior of herd animals when threatened?

Finally, in Chapter 8, we summarize the main findings. In that chapter, we also draw conclusions about the significant role of imitation in the life of humans. We hope you will enjoy this journey of how imitation behavior plays a role throughout our lives!

BOX 1.3 WHAT YOU SHOULD DEFINITELY REMEMBER FROM THIS CHAPTER

- Humans imitate a lot.
- Imitation is the basis for "social glue".
- Not only humans imitate, other animals do so too!
- Waiters around the world, thou shalt imitate and by doing so make a fortune.

NOTES

1 Lakin, J. L., Jefferis, V. E., Cheng, C. M., & Chartrand, T. L. (2003). The chameleon effect as social glue: Evidence for the evolutionary significance of nonconscious mimicry. *Journal of Nonverbal Behavior, 27*, 145–162. https://doi.org/10.1023/A:1025389814290

2 Van Baaren, R. B., Holland, R. W., Steenaert, B., & Van Knippenberg, A. (2003). Mimicry for money: Behavioral consequences of imitation. *Journal of Experimental Social Psychology, 39*, 393–398. https://doi.org/10.1016/S0022-1031(03)00014-3

3 Dickerson, K., Gerhardstein, P., Zack, E., & Barr, R. (2013). Age-related changes in learning across early childhood: A new imitation task. *Developmental Psychobiology, 55*, 719–732. https://doi.org/10.1002/dev.21068

4 Chartrand, T. L., & Bargh, J. A. (1999). The chameleon effect: The perception-behavior link and social interaction. *Journal of Personality and Social Psychology, 71*, 464–478. https://doi.org/10.1037/0022–3514.76.6.893

5 Ferrari, P. F., Visalbergi, E., Paukner, A., Gogassi, L., Ruggiero, A. & Suomi, S. J. (2006). Neonatal imitation in rhesus macaques. *PLoS Biology, 4*, 1501–1508. https://doi.org/10.1371/journal.pbio.0040302

2

THEORIES ON IMITATION

INTRODUCTION

Humans, of all times, like to imitate each other. In the 1930s, people looked at Hollywood stars for style inspiration. In the 1960s, almost every household was the proud owner of a lava lamp (see Figure 2.1). In the 1990s, "the Rachel haircut" was popular because women wanted to look just like Jennifer Aniston from the hit TV series *Friends*. And now, in the 2020s, supermarkets all over the globe experienced toilet paper shortages because people decided to

Figure 2.1 Lava lamp, popular in the 1960s.
Source: shutterstock.com.

DOI: 10.4324/9781003175056-2

buy the last roll "just in case" needed for a global pandemic (see Chapter 6 for a detailed explanation of this behavior). To express it lightly, humans are interesting beings.

In this chapter, we answer important questions about imitation. What is imitation? Why do humans copy each other? Who is likely to be copied? And lastly: is imitation rooted in the brain? Together, we will look at the *theories about imitation.*

WHAT IS IMITATION?

Before we can dive into the "why's and who's", it's important to first define what we mean by imitation. In Box 2.1, a definition of imitation is given, which was taken from the dictionary. For our purposes, Definition 1 and Definition 6 are most fitting. When we refer to imitation, we typically mean behavior that is *copied* by one person, after observing someone else doing this very behavior. Hence, two cognitive skills are required.[1] First, we need to be able and willing to *observe others*. Second, we need to be able and willing to *replicate* it.

BOX 2.1 DICTIONARY DEFINITION OF IMITATION

According to the Merriam-Webster dictionary, the definition of imitation (noun) is[2]:

1. An act or instance of imitating
2. Something produced as a copy: counterfeit
3. A literary work designed to reproduce the style of another author
4. The repetition by one voice of a melody, phrase, or motive stated earlier in composition by a different voice
5. The quality of an object in possessing some of the nature or attributes of a transcendent idea
6. The assumption of behavior observed in other individuals

There are two types of imitation: voluntary and automatic imitation.[3] Both will be covered in this book. *Voluntary imitation* is a conscious process: we decide to imitate someone else. For example, when we decide to buy a new brand of toothpaste simply because our favorite influencer brushes their teeth with it. *Automatic imitation* happens without the imitator being aware of it happening.

For example, when we automatically yawn upon seeing somebody else yawn. Unconscious imitation is typically called *mimicry* (we will talk about mimicry more later in this chapter).

Importantly, what we do *not* consider to be imitation? As you will see in this book, this is a difficult question. For now, we can say that the following cases do not concern imitation: synchronization and complementary behaviors.

Synchronization refers to different elements of a system working together as one coherent structure.[4] For example, in Figure 2.2, a group of birds is shown flying in a neat V-shape in a synchronized system: each bird is an element and together they make up the system. Humans can also make up systems together. For example, when a group of people collectively synchronize their behavior by chanting a song in a soccer stadium, marching in a parade, or dancing at a music festival. Although these people (the elements) are all doing the *same thing*, they are not necessarily imitating each other. They are synchronizing together, each human being one of the elements in the system. The birds flying in a V-shape, for example, are not necessarily imitating each other. Else, they might as well fly in conga line style. However, one could argue that in order to

Figure 2.2 Bird synchronization.
Source: shutterstock.com.

achieve synchronization, at least some elements of the system are imitating some of the behaviors from the other elements. Hence, the birds do need to start flying when they see the group taking off, or else they are left behind.

Complementary behaviors are also similar, yet different to imitational behaviors.[5] Here, two (or more) people complete each other's actions. Sometimes, both individuals make the exact same movement, making it look like imitation. For example, if your friend wants to shake your hand, they will reach out with their right hand. Thereafter, you do the exact same: you reach out your right hand. Hence, to someone unfamiliar with the concept of a handshake, it might look like you are copying your friend. However, you were *not* copying them. You were completing the action, initiated by your friend, ending in shaking each other's hands.

WHY DO WE IMITATE?

On to the next important question: why do humans imitate others? As briefly noted in Chapter 1, we think that there are two main motives behind imitation.

The first motive for imitation is learning. *Social learning* refers to learning by observing others or in interaction with others.[6] The general idea is that copying others allows people to avoid the "costs of learning". For example, if you want to figure out how to use the new printer at work, you can go ahead and figure it out yourself (trial and error) or read the lengthy instruction manual (learning by instruction). Both are very time consuming and require some effort from your side (the costs). However, if you simply watch your colleague using the printer and copy her step-by-step, it saves you time and energy.

The motive of learning is also relevant in "the zone of proximal development" (ZPD), a theory postulated by psychologist Vygotsky (see Chapter 4 for more details on this theory).[7,8] This zone is the difference between what someone can do by themselves and what someone can do under the guidance of a more capable person. The teenage son living next door, for example, cannot parallel park. But, under the guidance of his driver instructor, he can do the job. Hence, "parallel parking" is in his ZPD. Vygotsky thought that people could learn new skills best if they were in this zone. In the ZPD, people can learn best from others by copying their successful strategies.

The second motive is a social one. Everyone knows that imitation is the greatest form of flattery. Or at least that's what we like to tell ourselves when our coworker Andy "happens" to buy the exact same pair of shoes you got for your birthday last week. Hence, the second motive why people like to imitate is an effort to *gain approval* by others.[9,10] And often, this works too! (Not with Andy though).

Studies have shown that *mimicry* (which is automatic imitation, such as copying someone's yawn, smile, or posture) increases liking. Hence, the one being copied will like the copycat more. And, interestingly, there is a big mimicry-liking cycle: we mimic those we like more, which in turn leads them to like us more, and so on.[11,12] In line with this, there are plenty of studies showing positive effects of mimicry. Specifically, mimickers are more trusted, they are more likely to be answered when they ask a question, and they are even considered to be sexier.[13,14,15]

But what about Andy? Why is imitation sometimes *disliked*? There are also plenty of examples when imitation is flat-out annoying. For example, when a ten-year-old decides to repeat everything you say. One study suggests *awareness* might be the key factor here.[16] When we are aware someone is copying us, we don't like them more. But when we do not notice the copycat behavior, we will unconsciously pick up their mimicry and like them more. So, only sneaky copycats can rake in the benefits of imitation.

An influential psychological theory called the *optimal distinctiveness theory* is in line with the motive to gain approval. According to this theory, humans have two competing needs.[17] On the one hand, we have the need to be *included*, to be part of a social group, and to belong somewhere. On the other hand, we have the need to be *individuals*, to be unique. The first need (inclusiveness) drives us to copy others in the group. The second need (uniqueness) drives us to differentiate us from others. As both drives are at play and balance each other out, people aim for a level of "optimal distinctiveness". People strive to be like others, whilst maintaining a level of uniqueness. Thus, the motive to be *included* in a group (or to gain *approval by fellow group members*) can drive humans to imitation. But not only for humans it is important to blend in with the group. As you can see in Box 2.2, animals also use imitation for this.

BOX 2.2 WHAT CAN WE LEARN FROM ANIMALS' IMITATION BEHAVIOR?

Did you know that not only humans but most animals also imitate each other?[18] For example, yawning is contagious not only to humans but to dogs as well.[19] And infant chimpanzees, macaque monkeys, and orangutans will mimic the smiles of their adult counterparts, just like infant humans.[20,21] Animals too have several motives for imitation. A first motive is to *blend in with the group* to achieve safety. Predators are more likely to target individuals that stand out.

Hence, it is worth the effort for animals to blend in with the group. A second motive is to convey a *social message*. Just like humans, monkeys seem to like being imitated.[22] Finally, a third motive is *learning*. Like humans, animals can learn by watching others. This has been shown in many different animals such as birds, dogs, and monkeys. In these studies, animals, for example, learn how to use a lever to obtain food after watching another animal using it.

WHO DO WE IMITATE?

Now that we know why humans imitate others, let's look at who we like to imitate. After all, we do not just copy everyone and anyone we see, do we? There must be a reason why "the Rachel haircut" was popular, but nobody seems to be particularly interested in copying my hairstyle.

BOX 2.3 A BRIEF HISTORY OF PSYCHOLOGY: BEHAVIORISM VERSUS COGNITIVISM

About 150 years ago (to be exact, in 1879), something incredible happened to the world of science. Experimental psychology was born. It was in that year that Wilhelm Wundt established in Leipzig (Germany) the first laboratory to systematically study human behavior. The science of psychology was a fact. The history of science dates back much longer, arguably to the Ancient Greeks who practiced sciences like Medicine, Philosophy, and Astronomy, which also included the study of psychological concepts. Or maybe even further back to the Ancient Chinese who also practiced sciences like Physics, Philosophy and Chemistry. But Psychology as an official science is much younger than its brothers and sisters. This makes it such an interesting and fast-developing field!

Psychology aims to gather knowledge about humans: their thoughts (often called "cognitions") and behaviors. It didn't take very long for psychologists to start disagreeing with each other. One of the main focuses of the early debates was on the topic of learning: how do humans learn?

In one corner were the *behaviorists.*[23] Behaviorists liked to call the human mind a "black box" that could not be studied. In order to make psychology a "real science", psychologists ought to focus on factual observable behavior. They claimed all human behavior is learned through a mechanism called *conditioning.* There are two main types of conditioning. On the one hand, there is *classic conditioning.* The most famous example of this is the Pavlov reaction. If one rings a bell each time before giving dogs their food, soon the dogs will learn to associate the bell with receiving food. Hence, the dogs will drool all over the place when hearing the bell, even without getting any food. Humans can learn in this way as well. For example, if your dad baked a fancy chocolate cake each year for your birthday, you might come to associate the smell of chocolate cake with the happy feeling you got as a child on your birthday. Just smelling the cake is enough to relive those happy memories. The second form of conditioning is called *operant conditioning.* Here, we learn to associate things with its consequences: either rewards or punishments. For example, if we give a dog treat to puppies every time they sit, they will soon learn that sitting is good behavior. Hence, rewarded behavior will more likely happen again, and punished behavior will occur less.

In the other corner were the *cognitivists.* According to them, human behavior is learned through cognitive processes like attention, decision-making, and memory. Hence, they focus on the internal mental processes. Simply looking at humans as machines that can be trained was insufficient according to them. The mind is not a black box that needed be ignored, but it was the very thing they were interested in.

And luckily, in the 1960s, there was Albert Bandura. He came up with the *social learning theory.* This theory can be considered a bridge between the two opposing camps.[24] Bandura came up with the idea that we humans learn from observing others, which we call *model learning.* The basic idea is that by merely observing others, we can learn how to do it ourselves too. By watching others (a cognitive process), people can see what behavior is rewarded with success (akin to operant conditioning), internalize these (cognitive process), and try them out for themselves. In other words, Bandura described pure imitational learning (see Chapter 4 for more details on Bandura's theory).

As you can tell from Box 2.3, Bandura was the first to claim people can learn merely by observing others. But *who* are they more likely to learn from? Who are likely models?

Unsurprisingly, a first cue people look for is the *expertise of the model*.[25,26] People are more likely to imitate people who they think are experts rather than novices. From an evolutionary perspective, this makes a lot of sense. In deciding whom to copy, it is smart to copy those who are knowledgeable. So, when a teenager wants to copy someone's homework, they will most likely ask the top student of the class instead of an underperforming student. Sometimes, however, we imitate too much. For example, when young children (but also adults) learn a new skill, they tend to copy all the actions of the teacher, not only those actions that are relevant (see Box 2.4).

Now, let's look at the Rachel haircut. Why did women across the globe decide Jennifer Aniston was the one to copy? This is explained by the *prestige bias*.[27] Humans are more likely to imitate those who have obtained status. This too makes a lot of sense from an evolutionary perspective. Information about who is an expert is not always readily available. So, we must look at other cues. One of those cues is status, as it is an indirect marker of success. Status can be acquired and measured in many ways: for example, by being popular, rich, or being the boss. Unconsciously, we think "if everybody likes you, you must know what you are doing". So, we tend to imitate those who are popular more than those who are unpopular. Unfortunately, the prestige bias does have a dark side. For example, celebrity suicide often results in a wave of copycat suicide attempts by their fans (more on this in Chapter 5).[27]

A final cue we look for in deciding who to copy is the *likeness of the model*.[28] We are more likely to copy someone who is like us. Likeness can be defined in many ways: being of a similar age, the same ethnicity or perhaps having the same interests. But also spatial distance and time distance are at play: the closer someone is to you – literally – the more likely you are to copy them.[29]

BOX 2.4 WHEN TOO MUCH IS COPIED

The concept of *overimitation* has puzzled psychologists. Overimitation is the tendency young children have where they copy all actions by a model exactly, even those not relevant to reach their goal.[29,30] For example, when children watch an adult open a container whilst singing "*lalala*", the children might also sing when trying to open the container themselves. However, children do not always overimitate. Sometimes they only copy the exact behaviors needed to reach their goal (opening the container). Why is this? Some scientists think this has to do with the *goals* of the imitator.[31]

To reiterate, we described two broad motives: to gain *approval* by others and to *learn* efficiently. When children want to *learn* something new, they are more likely to only copy the actions needed to reach this goal. However, if they also want to affirm the social bond between them and the one they copy, they are more likely to overimitate. For example, children (and adults too) are more likely to imitate others when they make eye contact.[32]

The rise of modern-day influencers on social media is an excellent example of the *prestige bias* and *likeness bias* at play. Their prestige is easily measured: everyone can see how many followers, likes and dislikes, and even what famous friends influencers have. And, opposed to the "regular celebrity", influencers typically have a niche target group. Every subgroup has their own heroes, playing into the likeness factor. Gamers can look up to PewDiePie, makeup enthusiasts to Nikkie Tutorials, and foodies tune into Binging with Babish. Hence, their audience is tuned in specifically for their likeness to them. No wonder influencers are such effective marketing machines.

IS IMITATION ROOTED IN THE BRAIN?

What organs do we need to breathe? That's easy. Our lungs, right? Yes, but we also need our brain for breathing (the brain stem, an evolutionary speaking very old structure, oversees bodily functions such as breathing and heartbeat). That's because we need our brain for *all* behaviors. We need it for complex behaviors, such as solving difficult mathematical problems, but also for simple behaviors like breathing. Does this include imitational behaviors? The final question we like to answer in this chapter is "is imitation rooted in the brain?"

IMITATION WITHOUT THINKING

Earlier in this chapter, we briefly touched about touched on mimicry, promising to explain it in more detail later. Let's dive into it.

Mimicry is automatic and unconscious imitation.[33] By this, we mean that humans tend to copy others without even being aware of it. There are many examples available. Perhaps the most famous is the contagiousness of a yawn. When you see somebody else yawning, you can't help yourself and will yawn too. There are multiple "types" of mimicry.[34] The first category is *facial mimicry:* which is when someone copies the facial expressions of someone else. An example of this would be when you automatically smile back at somebody smiling to you. The second category is *emotional mimicry*, which is when you would copy someone's emotion. For example, if your friend is very happy about starting a new job, you might feel happy too. A third category is *behavioral mimicry*, where you would copy somebody's mannerisms, posture, or movements. For example, if you and two of your colleagues are talking outside discussing today's work and your colleagues put their hands in their pockets. Most likely, you will automatically do the same without even thinking about it! The final category is *verbal mimicry*, where you would copy somebody's words or way of speaking. For example, babies are inclined to cry when they hear another baby crying, which is a form of verbal mimicry. Another example would be if your partner is talking very fast and loudly, most likely, you will automatically do the same.

MIMICRY IN THE BRAIN

As described in Box 2.2, we humans are not the only ones engaging in mimicry. Many different animals tend to (automatically) copy each other as well. Hence, it isn't surprising that we know a lot about mimicry and how this looks like in the brain from animal studies.

In the 2010s, there was a big hype in the Psychology research field. Many researchers started to investigate the same topic: *mirror neurons*.[35] What are these? How are they related to imitation? And perhaps most importantly, was it worth the hype?

To understand what mirror neurons are, one first needs to know what neurons are. *Neurons* (also known as nerve cells) are cells in the brain and nervous system.[36] These cells function as little information messengers. They communicate using electrical pulses and chemical signals. The average adult brain has about 100 billion neurons. Typically, neurons in specific brain regions are active when you need that part of the brain to do a task. For example, if you are walking on a street, you need to activate the muscles in your legs. Thus, the brain regions responsible for this show activity.

Mirror neurons are a special type of neurons. These are active when we *observe someone else* doing something. Thus, our brain is mirroring the action. Simply watching somebody grab a cup will activate mirror neurons in our own brain that would be active when we would grab a cup ourselves!

Mirror neurons were first discovered in monkeys in the early 1990s. Interestingly, as the story goes, this was an accidental discovery. The researchers were investigating the activity of neurons in the monkey brains. The scientists used a technique called *single cell recording* (if you wonder why scientists use animals to learn about humans, please see Box 2.5). Here, the voltage (electrical charge) of one single neuron is measured. The monkeys had to press a switch to illuminate the content of a box, after which a door would open so the monkey could reach for the object in the box. Under each object was a small piece of food hidden for the monkeys to eat. Interestingly, the neurons were also active when the monkey remained still but merely watched the experimenter grasp the objects!

The scientists first looked at one area in the monkey brain (specifically, area F5 in the ventral premotor cortex, see also Figure 2.3). Later, mirror neurons were also found in other areas in the brain. Soon, human studies followed. Again, mirror neurons were found in various regions of the brain using single cell recording, and other brain imaging techniques such as magnetic resonance imaging (MRI) scanners (these machines you've likely seen in movies and TV series. Doctors use these machines to make images from patients' bodies. The machines use strong magnetic fields to obtain the images).

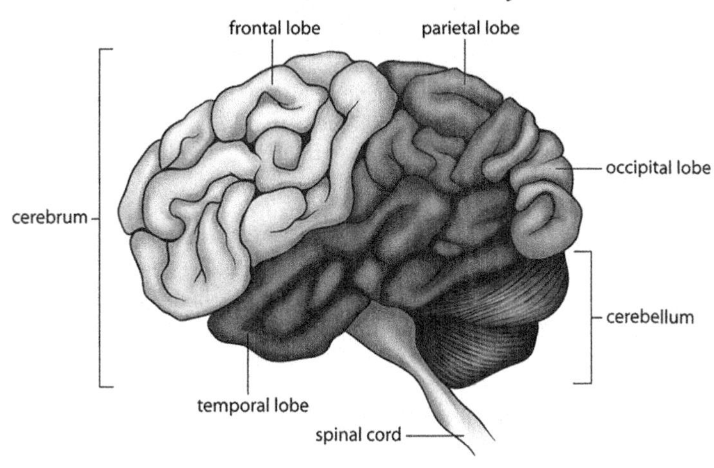

Figure 2.3 The human brain. Area F5 is located in the frontal lobe. This area of the brain contains "mirror neurons" which are involved in imitation.

Source: shutterstock.com.

Quickly, researchers got really excited. The mirror neurons were thought of as "mind reading cells",[37] which sounds very exciting. Different skills were related to mirror neurons: action understanding, speech and language, empathy, autism, and – most interesting to us – imitation.[38, 39] Overall, scientists agree that mirror neurons are indeed important for imitation.

BOX 2.5 ANIMAL BRAIN STUDIES

Why do scientists use animals to learn more about humans? First, we would like to acknowledge that there is a great ethical issue regarding animal studies. Obviously, animals cannot consent to participate in studies. Only (adult) humans can. And thus, many people believe we should refrain from studying animals altogether.

On the other hand, many important scientific breakthroughs have been reached *because* of animal studies. For example, in the 1920s, insulin was found to be an effective treatment of diabetes in dogs.[40]

And in the 1950s and 1960s, psychologists had major breakthroughs about the importance of attachment by studying infant rhesus monkeys.[41] Those in favor of animal studies conclude that these breakthroughs would never have happened without studying animals first and that the benefits thus outweigh the costs.

Putting this debate aside, we need to answer another important question: why is it even interesting to look at animal brains, if we can look at human brains? Well, the brains of mammals (such as humans, rats, cows etc.) are surprisingly like each other.[42] The main brain structures, and the connections between the different structures, are all relatively the same. Thus, by studying what brain regions are active in rats whilst eating sugar, we can infer that most likely the same areas are active in humans whilst eating sugar. Rats are much easier and cheaper to study than humans, and thus, scientist can more quickly test their theories.

WHAT CAN WE LEARN FROM BRAINS THAT WORK "DIFFERENTLY"?

Most people have "normal" brains (scientists like to use difficult terms, in this case "neurotypical brains"). Although everyone is a little different, our brains work in the same way. And most studies are conducted with people with standard brains.

However, nearly one in five persons has a mental disorder, permanently, or during a period in their lives.[43] This number includes many different disorders such as depression, autism, attention-deficit hyperactivity disorder (ADHD), or personality disorders. Many mental disorders are rooted in the brain.[44] Hence, these people are sometimes referred to as having *neurodivergent brains*. What can we learn about imitation from people with these "different functioning brains"?

Let's first look at people who show more imitation than the average person. An interesting group to look at are people with *autism spectrum disorder* (ASD). Most people with ASD struggle with social interactions. They show repetitive behaviors and/or can have very narrow interests.[45] One form of these repetitive behaviors in some people with ASD is *echolalia*.[46] Here, someone repeats a word or sentence someone else said repeatedly. For example, if Thomas's mom says, "Thommy, do you like the doggy?". Thomas could reply with "yes, doggy, doggy, doggy, doggy". Interestingly, people with ASD have also been identified as showing *less imitation*. Specifically, people with ASD are less inclined to display mimicry.[41, 47, 48]

Next to people with ASD, people with *social anxiety disorder* (SAD) also tend to show less mimicry.[49] People with SAD experience extreme fear in social settings. They do not enjoy social interactions and are instead preoccupied with their own performance ("Am I talking too fast?") and possible scrutiny by others ("They really don't like me, do they?"). It's quite interesting that people with SAD show less unconscious mimicry. As we've indicated above, there is a big mimicry–liking cycle. Hence, by not engaging in mimicry, the chances of the interaction partner liking you can decrease slightly, making them indeed look a little stern at you, making the already anxious person interpret it as hostile, and thus confirming and increasing their fears. In other words, they are trapped in a "less mimicry–less liking" cycle.

Regarding mimicry, another interesting group to look at are people with *borderline personality disorder* (BPD). These people generally struggle with mood swings, impulsive behaviors, maintaining relationships, and fear of abandonment. People with BPD can tend to focus on the negative side of things. They are more prone to pick up and interpret slight negative messages in a negative manner. For example, when someone is frowning at them, they interpret it as them being angry with them. They do the opposite with positive messages. For example, when someone is smiling at them, they are not that likely to interpret it as them liking them. In short, they are likely to think others dislike them or mean something in a negative way. And, as a result, they might feel very sad or angry themselves. Interestingly, this pattern is also found in their facial mimicry. People with BPD mimic more negative emotional displays (e.g., frowning) than positive emotional displays (e.g., smiling).[50]

Lastly, we turn to look at a syndrome where the nerves in the brain don't work properly: *Moebius syndrome*. People with this syndrome have very weak facial muscles, which can even completely paralyse. Hence, people with Moebius syndrome cannot show facial mimicry.[51] For a while, psychologists thought that facial mimicry might be necessary for people to recognize emotion. If someone cannot copy an emotion, one also cannot recognize what it means, they thought. But is this really the case? Studies on people with Moebius syndrome showed this is simply not true. Indeed, people with Moebius syndrome were equally good at recognizing emotions from facial expressions as people with typical brains! And this is thus even though they were not able to copy the facial expressions themselves.

BOX 2.6 WHEN WE DO NOT IMITATE

In order to fully answer the question "why do we imitate?", we should also ask ourselves the question: "why do we sometimes *not* imitate?". This is called *imitation inhibition* or *imitation control*. Imitation can be very useful – for example, when we want to know what flavor of ice cream to pick in a foreign country. Just go with whatever the person in front of you ordered, and you'll be good. But sometimes, we want to avoid it. For example, when imitation is considered rude (e.g., trying not to yawn during a presentation).

Scientists have looked at our brains when we try to combat our automatic imitation tendencies.[52] They found that areas in the brain that are generally active when we try to exert control are also active when trying to combat our automatic imitational response. In other words, the same brain regions needed to "not push a shiny red button" are needed to stop a contagious yawn.

CONCLUSION

In this chapter, we have discussed key theories related to imitation. These theories lay the basis for the following chapters. But as you will see, in the following chapters, additional relevant theories are also discussed. Sometimes, you might find yourselves browsing back to this chapter to read up on some context behind the findings. We started by defining imitation and differentiating it from similar concepts in psychology. We looked at theories on why we imitate. These can be summarized as follows: we want to learn and we want to be liked. To decide who to copy, we tend to look at how successful people are and how similar they are to us. This explains the power of the social media influencer. They work hard to portray they are "just like us" and have a built-in success meter in terms of followers, likes, and number of views. Next, we looked at how imitation looks like in the brain. Here, we focused mostly on automatic imitation called *mimicry*. Our brains have special cells – mirror neurons – that are active when we copy others. Lastly, we looked at people with neurodivergent brains, that is, people with different brains which may help us understand better what imitation is and what purpose it serves. For example, both people with autism and extreme social anxiety show less facial mimicry. These people struggle with social interactions. This suggests that imitation plays an important role in our relationships with other people. In conclusion, imitation is a broad topic with many interesting aspects to look at. While we have mostly discussed why humans (and other animals) imitate, in Box 2.6 we also briefly discuss why people do *not* imitate. In the following chapters, we will look at imitation across the human lifespan.

BOX 2.7 WHAT YOU SHOULD DEFINITELY REMEMBER FROM THIS CHAPTER

- Imitation is defined as behavior that is copied by one person, after observing someone else doing this very behavior.
- There are two motives for imitation: to learn and to gain social approval.
- There are two types of imitation: voluntary and automatic imitation. Voluntary imitation is a conscious process, and automatic imitation happens without the imitator being aware of it. The latter is also called *mimicry*.
- We have special nerve cells in the brain called mirror neurons that fire when we imitate others.
- Not everyone is equally likely to be copied. Those who are seen as experts, have status, or are very similar to the imitator are more likely to be copied.

NOTES

1 Rizzolatti, G. (2005). The mirror neuron system and imitation. In S. Hurley & N. Chater (Eds.), *Perspectives on imitation: From neuroscience to social science* (pp. 55–76). Cambridge, MA and London, England: The MIT Press.

2 Imitation. (2021). In *Merriam-Webster.com.* Retrieved October 14, 2021, from: https://www.merriam-webster.com/dictionary/imitation
3 Van Baaren, R. B., Decety, J., Dijksterhuis, A., Van der Leij, A., & Van Leeuwen, M. L. (2009). Being imitated: Consequences of nonconsciously showing empathy. *The Social Neuroscience of Empathy*, 31–42. https://doi.org/10.7551/mitpress/9780262012973.003.0004
4 Nowak, A., Vallacher, R. R., Zochowski, M., & Rychwalska, A. (2017). Functional synchronization: The emergence of coordinated activity in human systems. *Frontiers in Psychology, 8*, 945. https://doi.org/10.3389/fpsyg.2017.00945
5 Sartori, L., & Betti, S. (2015). Complementary actions. *Frontiers in Psychology, 6*, 557. https://doi.org/10.3389/fpsyg.2015.00557
6 Rendell, L., Boyd, R., Cownden, D., Enquist, M., Eriksson, K., Feldman, M. W., Fogarty, L., Ghirlanda, S., Lillicrap, T., & Laland, K. N. (2010). Why copy others? Insights from the social learning strategies tournament. *Science, 328*(5975), 208–213. https://doi.org/10.1126/science.1184719
7 Vygotsky, L. S. (1978). *Mind in society: The development of higher psychological processes.* Cambridge, MA: Harvard University Press.
8 Harland, T. (2003). Vygotsky's zone of proximal development and problem-based learning: Linking a theoretical concept with practice through action research. *Teaching in Higher Education, 8*(2), 263–272. https://doi.org/10.1080/13562510320000524 83
9 Parker-Rees, R. (2007). Liking to be liked: Imitation, familiarity and pedagogy in the first years of life. *Early Years, 27*(1), 3–17. https://doi.org/10.1080/13562510320000524 83
10 Duffy, K. A., & Chartrand, T. L. (2015). Mimicry: Causes and consequences. *Current Opinion in Behavioral Sciences, 3*, 112–116. https://doi.org/10.1016/j.cobeha.2015.03.002
11 Salazar Kämpf, M., Liebermann, H., Kerschreiter, R., Krause, S., Nestler, S., & Schmukle, S. C. (2018). Disentangling the sources of mimicry: Social relations analyses of the link between mimicry and liking. *Psychological Science, 29*(1), 131–138. https://doi.org/10.1177/0956797617727121
12 McIntosh, D. N. (2006). Spontaneous facial mimicry, liking and emotional contagion. *Polish Psychological Bulletin, 37*(1), 31–42. Retrieved from: http://www.communicationcache.com
13 Swaab, R. I., Maddux, W. W., & Sinaceur, M. (2011). Early words that work: When and how virtual linguistic mimicry facilitates negotiation outcomes. *Journal of Experimental Social Psychology, 47*, 616–621. https://doi.org/10.1016/j.jesp.2011.01.005

14 Guéguen, N., Martin, A., Meineri, S., & Simon, J. (2013). Using mimicry to elicit answers to intimate questions in survey research. *Field Methods, 25*, 47–57. https://doi.org/10.1177/1525822X12449710
15 Guéguen, N. (2009). Mimicry and seduction: An evaluation in a courtship context. *Social Influence, 4*, 249–255. https://doi.org/10.1080/15534510802628173
16 Kulesza, W., Dolinski, D., & Wicher, P. (2016). Knowing that you mimic me: The link between mimicry, awareness and liking. *Social Influence, 11*(1), 68–74. https://doi.org/10.1080/15534510.2016.1148072
17 Brewer, M. B. (1991). The social self: On being the same and different at the same time. *Personality & Social Psychology Bulletin, 17*(5), 475–482. https://doi.org/10.1177/0146167291175001
18 Bates, L. A., & Byrne, R. W. (2010). Imitation: What animal imitation tells us about animal cognition. *Wiley Interdisciplinary Reviews: Cognitive Science, 1*(5), 685–695. https://doi.org/10.1002/wcs.77
19 Harr, A. L., Gilbert, V. R., & Phillips, K. A. (2009). Do dogs (Canis familiaris) show contagious yawning? *Animal Cognition, 12*(6), 833–837. https://doi.org/10.1007/s10071-009-0233-0
20 Ferrari, P. F., Visalberghi, E., Paukner, A., Fogassi, L., Ruggiero, A., & Suomi, S. J. (2006). Neonatal imitation in rhesus macaques. *PLoS Biology, 4*(9), e302. https://doi.org/10.1371/journal.pbio.0040302
21 Davila-Ross, M., Menzler, S., & Zimmermann, E. (2008). Rapid facial mimicry in orangutan play. *Biology Letters, 4*(1), 27–30. https://doi.org/10.1098/rsbl.2007.0535
22 Paukner, A., Suomi, S. J., Visalberghi, E., & Ferrari, P. F. (2009). Capuchin monkeys display affiliation toward humans who imitate them. *Science, 325*(5942), 880–883. https://doi.org/10.1126/science.1176269
23 Cooper, P. A. (1993). Paradigm shifts in designed instruction: From behaviorism to cognitivism to constructivism. *Educational Technology, 33*(5), 12–19. Retrieved from: https://www.jstor.org/stable/44428049
24 Bandura, A. (1965). Influence of models' reinforcement contingencies on the acquisition of imitative responses. *Journal of Personality and Social Psychology, 1*(6), 589–595. https://doi.org/10.1037/h0022070
25 Meshi, D., Biele, G., Korn, C. W., & Heekeren, H. R. (2012). How expert advice influences decision making. *PLoS One*, 7(11), e49748. https://doi.org/10.1371/journal.pone.0049748
26 Jiménez, Á. V., & Mesoudi, A. (2019). Prestige-biased social learning: Current evidence and outstanding questions. *Palgrave Communications, 5*(1), 1–12. https://doi.org/10.1057/s41599-019-0228-7

27 Jeong, J., Do Shin, S., Kim, H., Hong, Y. C., Hwang, S. S., & Lee, E. J. (2012). The effects of celebrity suicide on copycat suicide attempt: A multi-center observational study. *Social Psychiatry and Psychiatric Epidemiology, 47*(6), 957–965. https://doi.org/10.1007/s00127-011-0403-7
28 Over, H., & Carpenter, M. (2012). Putting the social into social learning: Explaining both selectivity and fidelity in children's copying behavior. *Journal of Comparative Psychology, 126*(2), 182–192. https://doi.org/10.1037/a0024555
29 Hansen, J., Alves, H., & Trope, Y. (2016). Psychological distance reduces literal imitation: Evidence from an imitation-learning paradigm. *Journal of Experimental Psychology: Human Perception and Performance, 42*(3), 320–330. https://doi.org/10.1037/xhp0000150
30 Whiten, A., McGuigan, N., Marshall-Pescini, S., & Hopper, L. M. (2009). Emulation, imitation, over-imitation and the scope of culture for child and chimpanzee. *Philosophical Transactions of the Royal Society of London: Biological Sciences, 364,* 2417–2428. https://doi.org/10.1098/rstb.2009.0069
31 Carpenter, M., & Call, J. (2009). Comparing the imitative skills of children and nonhuman apes. *Revue de Primatologie, 1.* https://doi.org/10.4000/primatologie.263
32 Wang, Y., Newport, R., Hamilton, A. F. D. C. (2010). Eye contact enhances mimicry of intransitive hand movements. *Biology Letters,* 7(1), 7–10. https://doi.org/10.1098/rsbl.2010.0279
33 Wang, Y., & Hamilton, A. F. D. C. (2012). Social top-down response modulation (STORM): A model of the control of mimicry in social interaction. *Frontiers in Human Neuroscience, 6,* 153. https://doi.org/10.1098/rsbl.2010.0279
34 Duffy, K. A., & Chartrand, T. L. (2015). Mimicry: Causes and consequences. *Current Opinion in Behavioral Sciences, 3,* 112–116. https://doi.org/10.1016/j.cobeha.2015.03.002
35 Heyes, C., & Catmur, C. (2021). What happened to mirror neurons? *Perspectives on Psychological Science, 17,* 153–168. https://doi.org/10.1177/2F1745691621990638
36 National Institute of Neurological Disorders and Stroke (2019, December 16th). *Brain Basics: The Life and Death of a Neuron.* Retrieved on October 14th 2021 from: https://www.ninds.nih.gov/Disorders/Patient-Caregiver-Education/Life-and-Death-Neuron
37 Meltzoff, A. N., & Prinz, W. (Eds.). (2002). *The imitative mind: Development, evolution and brain bases* (Vol. 6). Cambridge: Cambridge University Press.
38 Iacoboni, M. (2009). Imitation, empathy, and mirror neurons. *Annual Review of Psychology, 60,* 653–670. https://doi.org/10.1146/annurev.psych.60.110707.163604

39 Williams, J. H., Whiten, A., Suddendorf, T., & Perrett, D. I. (2001). Imitation, mirror neurons and autism. *Neuroscience & Biobehavioral Reviews, 25*(4), 287–295. https://doi.org/10.1016/s0149-7634(01)00014-8
40 Karamitsos, D. T. (2011). The story of insulin discovery. *Diabetes Research and Clinical Practice, 93*, 2–8. https://doi.org/10.1016/S0168-8227(11)70007-9
41 Seay, B., Alexander, B. K., & Harlow, H. F. (1964). Maternal behavior of socially deprived Rhesus monkeys. *The Journal of Abnormal and Social Psychology, 69*(4), 345–354. https://doi.org/10.1037/h0040539
42 Neves, K., daCunha, F., & Herculano-Houzel, S. (2017) What are different brains made of? *Frontiers for Young Minds*. https://doi.org/10.3389/frym.2017.00021
43 National institute of Mental Health (n.d.). *Mental illness*. Retrieved on October 14th 2021 from: https://www.nimh.nih.gov/health/statistics/mental-illness
44 National Institutes of Health (NIH). (2007). *Information about mental illness and the brain*. In NIH curriculum supplement series. Retrieved from: https://www.ncbi.nlm.nih.gov/books/NBK20369/
45 American Psychiatric Association. (2013). *Diagnostic and statistical manual of mental disorders* (5th ed.). https://doi.org/10.1176/appi.books.9780890425596
46 Golysheva, M. D. (2019). A review on echolalia in childhood autism. *Advances in Social Science, Education and Humanities Research, 333*, 200–204. https://doi.org/10.2991/hssnpp-19.2019.37
47 Forbes, P. A., Pan, X., & Hamilton, A. F. D. C. (2016). Reduced mimicry to virtual reality avatars in autism spectrum disorder. *Journal of Autism and Developmental Disorders, 46*(12), 3788–3797. https://doi.org/10.1007/s10803-016-2930-2
48 Yoshimura, S., Sato, W., Uono, S., & Toichi, M. (2015). Impaired overt facial mimicry in response to dynamic facial expressions in high-functioning autism spectrum disorders. *Journal of Autism and Developmental Disorders, 45*(5), 1318–1328. https://doi.org/10.1007/s10803-014-2291-7
49 Vrijsen, J. N., Lange, W. G., Becker, E. S., & Rinck, M. (2010). Socially anxious individuals lack unintentional mimicry. *Behaviour Research and Therapy, 48*(6), 561–564. https://doi.org/10.1016/j.brat.2010.02.004
50 Matzke, B., Herpertz, S. C., Berger, C., Fleischer, M., & Domes, G. (2014). Facial reactions during emotion recognition in borderline personality disorder: A facial electromyography study. *Psychopathology, 47*(2), 101–110. https://doi.org/10.1159/000351122

51 Rives Bogart, K., & Matsumoto, D. (2010). Facial mimicry is not necessary to recognize emotion: Facial expression recognition by people with Moebius syndrome. *Social Neuroscience, 5*(2), 241–251. https://doi.org/10.1080/17470910903395692

52 Darda, K. M., & Ramsey, R. (2019). The inhibition of automatic imitation: A meta-analysis and synthesis of fMRI studies. *NeuroImage, 197*, 320–329. https://doi.org/10.1016/j.neuroimage.2019.04.059

3

IMITATION IN INFANCY

INTRODUCTION

Ten-month-old baby Maya sits in her high chair and eats a banana. Her dad is in the kitchen humming a song. Then he hears Maya sing along a bit. "Dadadadadada", sings Maya. Maya's dad walks up to her and says with a smile: "Very good Maya, dadadadadadadada". "Dada-dadadadada" Maya sings again, this time smiling broadly. Together they continue singing and Maya's dad gives her a big hug.

This chapter is about imitation in infancy. When babies are born, almost everything is new and strange to them. *Almost* everything, because the sounds and smells of their parents are of course familiar. In the first weeks and months, babies do not perceive people and objects around them in the way older children and adults do. For example, babies cannot see very well in the first weeks after birth, except when something (or someone) is very close to them. Their movements are still largely driven by reflexes. An example is the grasp reflex. If you touch a baby's hand with your finger, the baby will grasp your finger. A baby can do this without actually thinking about it. It is a reflex. But babies cannot perform many actions that older children and adults are totally used to, such as picking up a cup if they feel like having a drink. Also, more abstract things such as perception of time and space are not developed yet in small babies. The area of the brain that is responsible for this (which is called the "prefrontal cortex") is not yet sufficiently developed to understand these situations. For example, when dad leaves the room, a newborn is not aware that he is away. This realization develops when babies are around eight

DOI: 10.4324/9781003175056-3

to nine months old, the time when they first shows signs of *separation anxiety*.

Cultural norms, values, and customs are, of course, also completely foreign to newborn babies. How are you expected to behave in a public space, such as a museum, metro station, supermarket, or coffee bar? This is not something a baby tends to be knowledgeable (or care) about. Many parents will be familiar with a slight sense of embarrassment if their baby or toddler starts to scream very loudly in such a location. They would often try to communicate with the baby to stop the screaming, not always with much success... As we will see in Chapter 4, this is all information children will learn in the course of their development. Of course, also the language that is spoken in a culture is not familiar to babies. So, learning this language is a very important part of their socialization (see also Chapter 4). In sum, babies are very dependent on their environment to learn all these things. This means that, in addition to basics such as food and protection, babies also need tools to get to know the world around them and to be able to function well in it.[1]

Every child is born into a particular culture. This culture stimulates people to follow specific customs and traditions. Learning the culture and specific skills that are central to the culture (including language) is called *enculturation*. Imitation plays a very important role in enculturation. Consider Capoeira, which is a combination of a game, martial arts, and dance that is accompanied by music and comes from Brazil. How do you learn, for example, to do a complicated Capoeira move? By watching your older brother or sister and try to copy them. And how do you make the perfect dumpling? By watching while grandma prepares them and help her, which involves a lot of imitation. This type of learning is called *imitative learning*. It is universal among humans. Thus, this happens in every culture all over the world. As we will see in later chapters, imitative learning happens throughout our lives. But it is particularly important for learning new skills in infancy and childhood.

Because humans are able to transmit their culture to their offspring (see Chapter 1) – to a large part by means of imitation – the skills that are required to function well in that particular culture, the cultural traditions and habits, are established. Moreover, children tend to imitate their models (such as their parents, siblings, teachers, or peers) very carefully and even copy seemingly irrelevant actions. This is called *high-fidelity imitation* or *overimitation* (see also Chapter 2,

Box 2.4) and is only seen in humans, not in other animals. Why are humans doing this? The precise imitation of other people's actions is actually quite functional because it enables progress.

Once a certain action is learned by careful imitation, it can be further developed by others. Combined with some new discoveries and creative inventions, this leads to more and more complex societies. This building on each other's ideas is called *cumulative culture*. The mechanism through which this happens is called the *ratchet effect*. The term refers to a part of a machine that only allows movement in one direction. That is, it can only go forward (like progress) and not backward. In this sense, children further develop the skills of their parents, and their children, in turn, develop this even further and so on. As said, this is a characteristic only shown by humans and not by other animals. This is the reason that we humans can now press a button on our mobile phones to talk to (and see) someone who is located at the other side of the earth! Thus, imitation plays a large part in learning the culture, and through imitation, over generations, cultures further develop.

So, we have seen that *culture learning* is a first important function of imitation in infancy. A second important function of imitation in this phase is *affiliation*, or the creation and strengthening of a bond between the infant and their caregiver(s). Consider the example of baby Maya and her dad. It is clear that imitating each other, called *reciprocal imitation*, leads to positive and warm feelings between them.[2] Affiliation between a child and their caregiver is important because it promotes survival. Babies can obviously not survive on their own and therefore need the attention and love of others who can take care of them. Imitation stimulates affiliation between babies and their caregivers (Figure 3.1). But it is not only limited to direct caregivers such as parents. Imitation also strengthens feelings of affiliation between babies and other people around them, such as siblings, pedagogical employees at daycare, and peers. Importantly, it also works the other way around. Affiliation also affects imitation. For example, the type and quality of imitation differs between babies with and without siblings, as we will discuss later in this chapter.

In this chapter, we focus on imitation in infancy. We ask questions such as: Does imitation already occur in newborn babies? Or does it start later in infancy? Related to this, we ask the question: Is imitation innate or is it learned behavior? Along with that, we discuss *to what extent* babies imitate and *what* exactly they imitate. We will also further

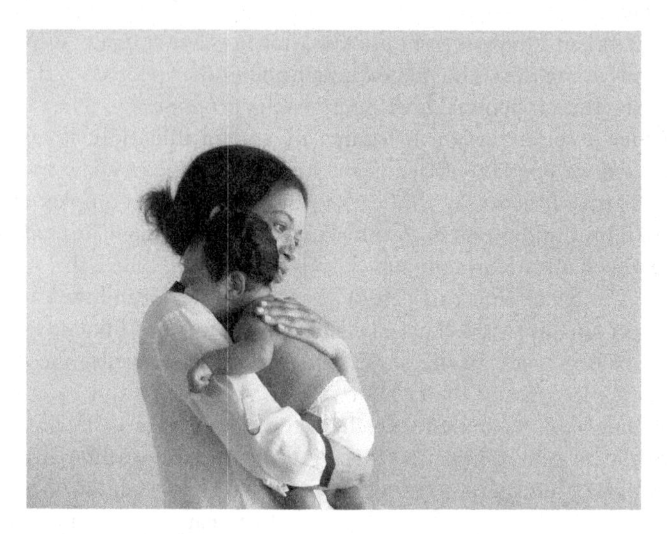

Figure 3.1 A mother comforting her child.
Source: Shutterstock.com.

explore the connection between imitation and affiliation at this age, as this is a very important aspect of future functioning of the individual in wider society. This is also related to the question *who* infants imitate and whether infants already assume a social motive in imitation. We end with a conclusion on imitation behavior in infancy.

DO NEWBORNS ALREADY IMITATE?

When do babies first show signs of imitation? This question is important because it is related to another question: Is imitation innate or is it learned? If babies are born with the ability to imitate someone else, then this would imply that imitation is innate. It is part of our genes we got from our parents. So, are all the necessary mechanisms and structures for imitation to occur already in place? If this would be the case, babies might show signs of imitation already a few hours after birth.

There is also another possibility. It could be that imitation is learned with age, for example, in interaction with others. In this case, one would not expect to see imitation right after birth. If babies only start to imitate later, say after a few months or even a year, this is evidence for the theory that the full ability to imitate is not innate. Of course, the capacity to develop imitation can be inherited and therefore innate. In other words, the necessary structures in the brain might exist at birth, just as is the case with the innate explanation. However, in this second explanation of imitation, the specific skills necessary to imitate will develop later and are at least partly learned, similar to language acquisition.

Two theories have been proposed to answer this question.[3] The first theory is the *nativistic account*. According to this theory, imitation is an innate ability (humans are born with it) that is already evident in newborns. This means that already at birth there is an inherited structure in the brain (the neurological system) that ensures that a baby can imitate. Researchers call this structure the *mirror system* (see also Chapter 2 on theories of imitation). The second theory about the origin of imitation, a *dynamic systems account*, states that babies cannot imitate right after they are born. This theory assumes that babies only learn to imitate later, in their second year of life, and that imitation further develops from there. According to this theory, imitation is therefore not innate. The mechanisms to learn through imitations may be there at birth, but the actual learning through imitation does not become "active" until later in infancy.

Which of these ideas is correct? Before we answer this question, we will explain why knowledge about this issue is so important. We (the writers of this book) are not the first ones to show an interest in the origin of imitation in human beings. The question of whether imitation is innate or learned has dominated heated debate among researchers for several decades. This is because the answer to this question has large implications. Consider this: if imitation is innate and already present right after birth that would mean that humans inherit a lot of skills that are immediately available to us directly after we are born! They have to be able to clearly see another person's behavior (are the eyes already able to see it?), have an idea of their own body and how to use it *and* decide to imitate the model's behavior (is the brain working properly already?), and finally have to perform the imitating behavior (is the body already able to do this?). If, on the other hand, imitation is learned later on, this means the capacity to learn those skills – and perhaps also the motivation to learn them – might be present at birth, but the skills themselves still have to develop. For example, they could be learned through social interaction with caregiver or siblings.[4]

Knowing which one of these alternatives (innate imitation versus learned imitation) is true is, of course, by itself interesting. It is also important because it relates more generally to the question where human knowledge comes from. This question is a core issue in the field of cognitive development.[5] Very generally, cognitive development is the development of the way people think and perceive their surroundings. More insight in the origin of imitation may thus contribute to what we know about innate (versus learned) human abilities in general. It also helps further theory building in the domains of social (how we interact with our environment) and cognitive (how we perceive the environment) development.[6] In short, the answer to the innate-learned question can have implications for areas with regard to social learning that are related to (and might build further on) imitation skills, such as empathy, cooperation, and language.[7]

EMPIRICAL EVIDENCE FOR IMITATION IN NEWBORNS

So, what does science say about this issue? Many researchers have empirically investigated the "imitation is innate versus imitation is learned" question in the past few decades. The Swiss developmental psychologist Jean Piaget (1896–1980) is well known for his theory about children's cognitive development. He was interested in the question how children perceive their environment and interact with it. He conducted a number of studies where he observed children performing some tasks that he developed. Some of these studies he carried out with his own children Jacqueline, Laurent, and Lucienne. Based on his observations, Piaget thought that imitation is not innate but learned.[8]

Piaget described three stages in the process of learning to imitate in infancy: *absence of imitation*, *sporadic imitation*, and the start of *systematic imitation*. So, if we follow Piaget's research, this implies that imitation is something that is acquired after birth and is not innate. In other words, young infants develop the skills to imitate only later on in life. However, after Piaget, other researchers conducted studies that showed some evidence for the innate account.[9] These studies showed that babies can actually imitate other people's gestures, facial expressions, and sounds already right after birth. This idea that newly born babies are already able to imitate was generally accepted for some decades in the second half of the 20th century. But from then onward, the scientific evidence – or more accurately the lack of evidence – shifted back to the direction of the "imitation is learned argument". How did researchers arrive at this point?

In 1977, a seminal and controversial study was published in the prestigious journal *Science*.[10] In this study, it was found that infants aged 12–21 days old can already imitate facial gestures such as tongue protrusion and mouth opening. It also showed some evidence that children can imitate manual gestures, such as finger movements. Because this is such a well-known and often-cited study, we will describe it in more detail here.

The study consisted of two experiments. In the first experiment, six infants (three male and three female) who were 12–17 days old were tested as follows: first the babies saw a male experimenter who kept his face completely neutral for 90 seconds. He showed a "passive face". Then, in a 15-second "stimulus presentation period", each baby saw one of the following gestures four times in a row: lip protrusion, mouth opening, tongue protrusion, or sequential finger movement (opening and closing the hand by serially moving the fingers). After these 15 seconds, the experimenter again showed a passive face for 20 seconds. Then the same was done with one of the other gestures. Between the various gestures, the passive face was shown for 70 seconds. The babies were shown the gestures in a different random order. For example, one baby saw tongue protrusion first, another baby saw mouth opening first, and so on. Sometimes the babies did not watch carefully (because babies don't always cooperate!). In such cases, the gesture was repeated (up to three times). This was all videotaped and then coded by undergraduate volunteers. These coders indicated which gestures shown to the babies they thought were most likely imitated by the baby.

The second experiment, which involved 12 babies, controlled for a possible bias. A bias is something that may influence the results of a study outside the control of the experimenter. In this case, the bias could have been that the person who interacted with the baby actually adjusted their behavior based on the baby's response. So, for example, if the baby showed some indication that she started opening her mouth, the adult model (unconsciously) opened his mouth in response. This bias was controlled for using the "pacifier technique". The experimenter inserted a pacifier into the infants' mouth during the demonstration of the target behavior. In that way, the experimenter would not (unconsciously) adjust their gesture as a result of the infants' imitative response. This technique also ensured that the baby had actually seen the behavior.

The results of both experiments showed that the babies matched the gestures shown by the model. So, if the model protruded their lips, the babies also protruded their lips (according to the coders). Instead, if the model opened their mouth, the babies also opened their mouth, and so on. The researchers therefore concluded that this type of imitation is likely innate. It is already present at birth and not acquired later in life (see Box 3.1 for some considerations about this type of research).

Later, some researchers were critical about the findings of this study. For example, an article from 2009 compared multiple studies on imitation in infants from birth until two years of age.[11] In particular, the evidence for the two previously mentioned theories to explain the origin of imitation, the *nativistic account* (the ability to imitate is present at birth) and the *dynamic systems account* (the ability to imitate develops only later in life), is reviewed. It is concluded that most of the existing evidence until then was in line with the dynamic systems account. In other words, imitation is not innate but learned. This point of view is substantiated by the fact that there is little evidence of imitation among newborns of behaviors other than tongue protrusion. Even more importantly, it is shown that the findings in the studies on newborn imitation can be explained in different ways.[12] For example, it is quite possible that if an infant sees someone sticking out their tongue, they experience interest or arousal and as a result of this arousal stick out their tongue themselves. So, the match – adult sticks out tongue, baby sticks out tongue – is not imitation in this case, but pure coincidence! Thus, an important alternative explanation for the findings of newborn imitation is the so-called *arousal explanation* (see also Box 3.1).

BOX 3.1 DOING RESEARCH WITH INFANTS

Research with babies is difficult because you cannot ask them directly for their thoughts, motivations, or feelings. So, a lot of what you measure is indirect. Measuring something in an indirect way means that it is inferred from certain actions, such as the time an infant looks at certain stimuli. Furthermore, babies don't listen so well to instructions and usually (try to) do what they feel like at that particular moment. In addition, there are other things that make research with babies challenging.[13] For example, how do you know whether a baby's response to a model is really imitation or whether it is just general arousal? The baby can't tell you the answer.

Suppose an adult sticks out their tongue a number of times and the baby sticks out their tongue too. When you repeat this a number of times and the baby tends to stick out the tongue more often than when the model does nothing, then this would suggest that the baby is imitating the adult. However, tongue protruding, as it is called, can also simply be a response to a moving face, that is, the baby is more inclined to stick out their tongue when they see a moving face. So, it does not have to be imitation. A solution to this problem is to test multiple similar gestures. So besides sticking out the tongue several times, the adult also opens the mouth multiple times. If the baby still sticks out the tongue when the adult opens their mouth, then this would suggest that the baby is not imitating the adult. However, if the baby starts opening the mouth when the model opens the mouth, then this would be evidence for imitation.

Another obstacle in this type of research may be bias on the part of the experimenter (the model) and the coders (the persons responsible for counting the baby's reactions). If they already know what is being investigated, they can unconsciously act more in line with the expected outcome of the study. This is called the *experimenter effect*. In this case, the expectation is that babies imitate the models so models and coders might, for example, be more inclined to indeed spot this imitation behavior in the babies. As a result, coders might code the baby's reactions more in line with the expected outcomes of the study. This is especially likely to occur when the baby's response is not very clear. For example, it is not clear whether the baby sticks out their tongue or just licks their lips. Researchers try to prevent these biases by not telling the models and the coders about the expected results of the study. Also, they receive an extensive training beforehand.

Over time, the techniques to study imitation behavior in babies have become more advanced. For example, in studies on this topic, computer-animated characters have been used as stimuli. The advantage of this is that the coders were blind to the research question. In other words, they are not affected by the expected outcomes of the study. If an experimenter is also the model who performs a certain action to see whether the baby imitates it, they are aware of what is being studied. This can create a bias in their behavior and therefore influence the results of the study. However, when computer animations are used, this problem is solved. Another important advantage is that the sessions in such experiments can be completely standardized. This means that only the behavior that is studied (in this particular case, imitative and affiliative behavior) is manipulated by the experimenter. Even if you train experimenters very well to model in exactly the same way, the different trials will never be completely similar. Maybe the experimenter is more tired in the tenth trial than in the first one. Or they have to go to the bathroom! This influences their behavior. Therefore, an experiment using computer-animated stimuli is less biased than an experiment with real human models performing the behavior.

Empirical evidence for this arousal explanation was, for example, found in a study with four-week-old infants. They listened for 20 seconds to Rossini's *Barber of Seville Overture*. They stuck out their tongue more often in 20-second silent breaks after the music.[14] The music was "chosen for the potentially arousing quality of its numerous changes in tempo, pitch, and volume" (p. 128). This shows that when babies perceive (in this case, hear) something that they find interesting, they tend to stick out their tongue. So, it may have been the case that the babies in the study described above were simply interested in what was happening around them, instead of reacting specifically to the protracted tongue.

In the following years, more evidence arose that supports the argument that imitation is learned. For example, in 2011, researchers reviewed a number of previous studies about imitation among newborns.[15] They found very few evidence that imitation is already present right after birth. Finally, in a large longitudinal study (a study in which children were observed at different moments over time) from 2016, also no evidence for imitation at this young age was found.[16] In this study, the researchers looked at the responses of 106 newborns at different ages (one, three, six, and nine weeks) to different gestures at different times. Some gestures were shown by human models: tongue protrusion, mouth opening, a happy face, and a sad face. The researchers also made use of nonhuman objects which portrayed facial gestures, for example, a spoon protruding through a tube and a box opening. Another object looked like a hand gesture of the index finger protrusion. Yet another object resembled a hand grasping for something. Also, three vocal gestures were played ("mmm", "eee", and "click" sounds).

The researchers counted the number of times the infants showed each of the different gestures when viewing the models. So they were able to compare the number of times the infants showed a matching response to the model with the number of times they showed that same response to other gestures shown by the model. If the infant would, for example, stick out their tongue more often after the model did so than after the model did something else, this would be evidence for imitation. Again, no evidence for any type of imitation was found. The babies were equally likely to produce matching and nonmatching behaviors in response to models' gestures. These researchers therefore also concluded that imitation is not an innate ability but learned in the first years of our lives.

OK, so it is settled you might think, babies do not imitate right after birth. Imitation develops later in infancy. Well, it is not that clear unfortunately. First, the researchers of the famous 1970s study published in the scientific journal *Science* did not agree with the 2016 study we just described. They published a rebuttal (this is a response to another article) identifying several flaws in the later study. They also claimed that the data actually *do* support the imitation of tongue protrusion in early infancy. In turn, the 2016 researchers responded to the 1970s researchers by refuting their claims, and they ended their argument with the following statement: "Until more compelling evidence emerges, however, a propensity to imitate from birth should no longer be considered an established phenomenon."[17] (p. 2). As you can see, the debate is ongoing and the topic remains highly controversial. However, the idea that imitation is a very important mechanism that plays a role in cognitive and social development, and through which infants learn their culture, is acknowledged by all of them.

AFFILIATION AND IMITATION IN INFANCY

As already mentioned in the Introduction section, affiliation, a strong physical and emotional bond between babies and their caregivers, is very important for a healthy development. This is important during childhood in general, but it is in particular important when babies are very small. Naturally, without the care of their parent(s) or other caregiver(s), babies would not be able to survive. Moreover, food, warmth, and shelter are not enough for a baby to develop healthily and become an adult who can function well in society. So babies and children need psychological warmth and love for a healthy social–emotional development. *Attachment theory*, a landmark theory developed by the psychiatrist John Bowlby (1907–1990), explains how children who are neglected at their young age may become detached and experience many psychological problems later in life. But what role does imitation play in affiliation? First, imitation can be considered an affiliative act in itself that fosters (social) learning. Two imitation scholars put it as follows:

> Imitation is a universal language for expressing social engagement, because one can only systematically imitate the behavior of another person if one is attending to that person. If the imitated behavior serves no clear instrumental function, moreover, then its performance suggests that the imitator is motivated not only to attend to the target of imitation but to align with the target for social or communicative purposes (p. 31).[18]

So imitation is, first of all, a sign of affiliation. Next to that, imitation may also (further) stimulate affiliation between a baby and its caregiver. The example of baby Maya and her dad described in the Introduction of this chapter is an illustration of such an imitative interaction that could lead to interpersonal bonding. Interestingly, in these interactions, the infant may also recognize that someone else (e.g., the caregiver) is imitating them. That is, it performs a certain behavior and then sees the other doing the same. The baby is recognizing that the other is acting "like-me". It is theorized that this experience of others acting "like-me" could be the basis of more complex social cognitive abilities. So, in this view, it is not only the infant imitating others but also the infant recognizing that others are imitating them, that is important for learning and development.[19]

Imitation can occur in different ways: we can imitate on an instructional basis. This means that a "model" (a parent, teacher, friend, or sibling) performs an act and gives an explanation on how to perform this act. But imitation can also happen without instructions, so spontaneously. There is evidence that particular relations between people facilitate this type of spontaneous imitation. For example, in one study parents were asked to observe and record the imitation behavior of their infants.[20] The infants were 12–18 months old. Some of the infants had one or more older siblings, and others had no siblings.

In general, parents reported that their infants imitated, on average, about three behaviors per day. Of these behaviors, about one was novel behavior that the parents had never seen them perform before. So this is a clear and real-world demonstration of how infants learn by imitating. This is an important finding, especially because this study focused on natural behavior of children in their own surroundings. Many studies on imitation with infants and children are done in a laboratory which is much less natural, of course. Results of real-life studies such as these are therefore important because they reflect our daily life much better and can be compared with results from the laboratory studies.

Interestingly, in this study, it was also found that the infants with siblings imitated more behavior spontaneously, so without them being explicitly instructed, than infants without siblings. Infants without siblings imitated more instructed behavior than infants with siblings. So it is clear that *how* infants imitate differs depending on *who* the infant is imitating, which actually depends on who is around. It is not clear though whether spontaneous imitation without instruction fosters better or faster learning than imitation with instruction. If that would be the case, that would mean that infants with (older) siblings would learn some things better or faster than infants without siblings. But maybe there are also benefits of imitation that is instructed over imitation that is spontaneous. Maybe instructed imitation promotes a different type of learning? We do not know the answers to these questions yet, so this would be an interesting avenue for future research.

Another remarkable finding in this study concerned the *type* of behavior the infants imitated. This behavior generally ranged from sounds and gestures such as waving, clapping, or stamping the feet, to play such as riding a bike, doing "peek-a-boo", or engaging in joined pretend play (see Chapter 4). Infants also imitated routines such as cleaning, feeding pets, or answering the telephone. However, it was found that infants with siblings imitated more play behaviors, specifically rough-and-tumble play (climbing, jumping, chasing) and joined pretend play, than infants without siblings. By the way, infants not only imitated other humans such as their parents or siblings but also imitated nonhuman objects, such as the dishwasher, and animals, such as the dog which ate food off the floor! Infants also imitated actions they saw on television. This was actually the most frequently coded "model", besides adults or children around them. In particular, the finding that infants with siblings showed more joined pretend play than infants without siblings could be important with regard to children's development. This is because joined pretend play has been associated with cognitive skills such as problem solving, creativity, and the development of a *theory of mind* (see Chapter 4 on theory of mind) (Figure 3.2).[21]

We have talked about what and who infants imitate. But in the context of affiliation, it would also be interesting to find out what happens when infants observe imitative behavior performed by others. How do they interpret this behavior? For example, do they (already) have the ability to guess what motivates people when they imitate others? Research with babies of different ages focused on this question.[22]

In a first set of experiments, 4–5.5-month-old babies were placed in a car seat in front of a display screen. The screen showed a number of computer-animated characters (circles with a smiling face) who copied the behavior – sounds or movements such as jumping – of other characters. In the sessions, the babies were also presented with characters who did *not* copy the behavior of the other

Figure 3.2 A baby girl who engages in pretend play of food with her toys.
Source: shutterstock.com.

characters. So the baby's response to the characters that did and the characters that did not imitate could be compared. After the babies saw the character imitating or not imitating the other characters, the target character approached the others and then moved together with them (synchronization). So, in one situation, the character imitated and then showed affiliation – this was called the *congruent session*. In the other situation, the character did *not* imitate and then showed affiliation – the *incongruent session*.

Importantly, the babies were filmed while looking at the screen. The time that they looked at the screen during each session was measured by experimenters who were unaware of what the babies had seen. By the way, some of the data of these little participants had to be excluded because of fussiness or inattentiveness. Again, we see that babies are not the easiest participants!

The results showed that the babies looked longer at the screen when they saw the congruent event than when they saw the incongruent event. The researchers interpreted this longer looking time as evidence that the babies could distinguish between the congruent and incongruent events. This could mean that the babies were more motivated to look at the congruent event because they were trying to confirm an expectation that imitators are likely to show affiliation to the ones they have imitated. But how can we be so sure of this explanation? Do the findings indeed mean that babies at such a young age already make a connection between imitation and affiliation?

The answer to these questions is difficult because, as mentioned before, we cannot ask the babies why they looked longer at the congruent events. And there are other possible explanations for the findings than the one proposed by the researchers. It could, for example, be the case that infants looked longer at congruent events because they preferred behavior that is more familiar. As the congruent event showed the same behavior twice, instead of only once in the incongruent event, that behavior is more familiar. By using a number of follow-up experiments in which the researchers varied certain elements, they tried to find the reason for the longer looking time after imitation–affiliation than after non-imitation–affiliation. For example, in another experiment, it was not the characters who imitated (or did not imitate) the others who showed affiliation, but the characters *who were imitated* (and those who were not imitated) who showed affiliation. In other words, this concerned the affiliative behavior of potential *targets* of imitation. In this case, the babies looked equally long at congruent and incongruent events.

So, babies were only motivated to look longer at situations in which affiliation followed imitation if this concerned the imitator and not if it concerned the target of imitation. Thus, the "familiarity-explanation" explained above can be ruled out. The results could instead indicate that babies interpret imitation as a type of social behavior that predicts affiliation. Interestingly, according to the authors, "these findings suggest that imitation has social significance for infants, at an age when infants' own imitative skills are limited (p. 45)." The possibility that children at such a young age can already connect imitation and affiliation could be an indication of the importance of social learning for children and humans in general.

CONCLUSION

Babies are very interesting to study. They are also quite difficult to study. They cannot explain to us their motivations, and they often do what they want in a given situation. This makes studying imitation in infancy particularly challenging. But we do know that imitation is very important already in infancy. It is a mechanism through which babies and children learn their culture. In addition, it plays a role in creating a bond between the infant and others around them, most importantly, their caregivers. An important question is: *When* do babies actually start imitating others? Are they able to imitate right after birth or do they learn this only later in life? In other words, is imitation innate or is it learned? In this chapter, we discussed some of the studies that have been done in this area. We have seen that the topic is controversial, and the discussion caused (and still causes) strong disagreement among developmental scientists. Although the current evidence seems to favor the idea that imitation is not innate but learned, the last word has not yet been said about the issue. Future research will need to shed more light on this fascinating question. We have also discussed the research that shows that imitation and affiliation are strongly linked. Babies imitate in a different way depending on who is around (e.g., siblings), and they also seem to be inclined to connect imitation to affiliation in interactions between others. Clearly, imitation is a very important skill that is central to people's social life and that starts to develop already early in life.

BOX 3.2 WHAT YOU SHOULD DEFINITELY REMEMBER FROM THIS CHAPTER

- Two functions of imitation in infancy are learning the culture, called enculturation, and affiliation, meaning creating and strengthening the bond between babies and their parents, caregivers, siblings, peers and others.
- There has been a heated debate around the question whether imitation is innate or whether it is learned. The most recent evidence is leaning towards the "learned-argument". Babies do not seem to have the ability to imitate right after birth. Rather, they learn it during the course of infancy and childhood.
- The presence of siblings is important for how babies imitate (spontaneous or instructed) and for the type of imitation they show (more rough-and-tumble play and more joined pretend play than babies without siblings).
- Babies already seem to be able to connect imitation to affiliation when they see it in others.

NOTES

1 Meltzoff, A. N., & Marshall, P. J. (2018). Human infant imitation as a social survival circuit. *Current Opinion in Behavioral Sciences*, *24*, 130–136. https://doi.org/10.1016/j.cobeha.2018.09.006

2 Meltzoff, A. N., & Marshall, P. J. (2018). Human infant imitation as a social survival circuit. *Current Opinion in Behavioral Sciences*, *24*, 130–136. https://doi.org/10.1016/j.cobeha.2018.09.006

3 Jones, S. S. (2009). The development of imitation in infancy. *Philosophical Transactions of the Royal Society B: Biological Sciences*, *364*(1528), 2325–2335. https://doi.org/10.1098/rstb.2009.0045

4 Ray, E., & Heyes, C. (2011). Imitation in infancy: The wealth of the stimulus. *Developmental Science*, *14*(1), 92–105. https://doi.org/10.1111/j.1467-7687.2010.00961.x

5 Jones, S. S. (2009). The development of imitation in infancy. *Philosophical Transactions of the Royal Society B: Biological Sciences*, *364*(1528), 2325–2335. https://doi.org/10.1098/rstb.2009.0045

6 See for example Meltzoff, A. N., & Moore, M. K. (1977). Imitation of facial and manual gestures by human neonates. *Science*, *198*(4312), 75–78. https://doi.org/10.1126/science.198.4312.75

7 Heyes, C. (2016). Imitation: Not in our genes. *Current Biology*, *26*(10), R412–R414. https://doi.org/10.1016/j.cub.2016.03.060

8 Piaget J. (1962). *Play, dreams and imitation in childhood.* New York: Norton. Translated from French. First English edn. Published 1951.

9 Meltzoff, A. N., & Moore, M. K. (1977). Imitation of facial and manual gestures by human neonates. *Science, 198*(4312), 75–78. https://doi.org/10.1126/science.198.4312.75
10 Meltzoff, A. N., & Moore, M. K. (1977). Imitation of facial and manual gestures by human neonates. *Science, 198*(4312), 75–78. https://doi.org/10.1126/science.198.4312.75
11 Jones, S. S. (2009). The development of imitation in infancy. *Philosophical Transactions of the Royal Society B: Biological Sciences, 364*(1528), 2325–2335. https://doi.org/10.1098/rstb.2009.0045
12 See Jones, S. S. (2009). The development of imitation in infancy. *Philosophical Transactions of the Royal Society B: Biological Sciences, 364*(1528), 2325–2335. https://doi.org/10.1098/rstb.2009.0045
13 See Meltzoff, A. N., & Moore, M. K. (1977). Imitation of facial and manual gestures by human neonates. *Science, 198*(4312), 75–78. https://doi.org/10.1126/science.198.4312.75
14 Jones, S. S. (2006). Exploration or imitation? The effect of music on 4-week-old infants' tongue protrusions. *Infant Behavior and Development, 29*(1), 126–130. https://doi.org/10.1016/j.infbeh.2005.08.004
15 Ray, E., & Heyes, C. (2011). Imitation in infancy: The wealth of the stimulus. *Developmental Science, 14*(1), 92–105. https://doi.org/10.1111/j.1467-7687.2010.00961.x
16 Oostenbroek, J., Suddendorf, T., Nielsen, M., Redshaw, J., Kennedy-Costantini, S., Davis, J., … & Slaughter, V. (2016). Comprehensive longitudinal study challenges the existence of neonatal imitation in humans. *Current Biology, 26*(10), 1334–1338. https://doi.org/10.1016/j.cub.2016.03.047
17 Oostenbroek, J., Redshaw, J., Davis, J., Kennedy-Costantini, S., Nielsen, M., Slaughter, V., & Suddendorf, T. (2018). Re-evaluating the neonatal imitation hypothesis. *Developmental Science*, 22(2), e12720. https://doi.org/10.1111/desc.12720
18 Powell, L. J., & Spelke, E. S. (2018). Human infants' understanding of social imitation: Inferences of affiliation from third party observations. *Cognition, 170*, 31–48. https://doi.org/10.1016/j.cognition.2017.09.007.
19 Meltzoff, A. N., & Marshall, P. J. (2018). Human infant imitation as a social survival circuit. *Current Opinion in Behavioral Sciences, 24*, 130–136. https://doi.org/10.1016/j.cobeha.2018.09.006
20 Barr, R., & Hayne, H. (2003). It's not what you know, it's who you know: Older siblings facilitate imitation during infancy. *International Journal of Early Years Education, 11*(1), 7–21. https://doi.org/10.1080/0966976032000066055
21 See Barr, R., & Hayne, H. (2003). It's not what you know, it's who you know: Older siblings facilitate imitation during infancy. *International Journal of Early Years Education, 11*(1), 7–21. https://doi.org/10.1080/0966976032000066055.
22 Powell, L. J., & Spelke, E. S. (2018). Human infants' understanding of social imitation: Inferences of affiliation from third party observations. *Cognition, 170*, 31–48. https://doi.org/10.1016/j.cognition.2017.09.007

IMITATION IN CHILDHOOD

INTRODUCTION

Have you ever wondered why toy stores are filled with miniature household equipment? A miniature version of a vacuum cleaner (that sadly does not even work!), a small kitchen (complete with fake food and fake knives), and even a tiny washer dryer can be bought for your little ones at home. Given that we don't really like the adult versions all too much (it cannot be just us dreading the laundry pile at the end of each week), why do children like these toys so much? The answer is, once again, imitation! Children enjoy imitating the adults they see in their everyday life. But why is this the case? This chapter dives into what is known about imitation in childhood.

"DEAR SANTA, I WANT A VACUUM FOR CHRISTMAS!"

Children enjoy imitating others. This form of play is called *pretend play* (see also Chapter 3). Pretend play is an activity one engages in that has no immediate goal, other than having fun.[1] There are many forms of play children engage in. For example, in constructive play, children build things. Playing with Legos, building a fortress out of bed sheets, and playing with magnetic blocks all fall under this category. Pretend play involves acting as-if. The behaviors within the game are not meant to reflect reality.[2] The examples range from a one-year-old pretending a banana is a telephone to a six-year-old running around in a superhero costume to a child asking Santa for "a vacuum" (cleaner) for Christmas (see Figure 4.1). There is one key ingredient in this type of play: imagination.

DOI: 10.4324/9781003175056-4

Figure 4.1 "A vacuum" (cleaner) for Christmas.
Source: shutterstock.com.

WHEN SHOULD YOU BUY YOUR KID A SUPERHERO COSTUME?

To answer this question, you should know about what forms of pretend play there are and at what age children engage in these forms of pretend play (see Table 4.1 for an overview). Children first engage in pretend play when they are 12–18 months old. Typically, they engage in a relatively simple form of pretend play called *object substitution*. This happens when the child pretends an object has a different function,[3, 4] for example, pretending a banana is a telephone, a spoon is an airplane, or your sock is a monster. Soon though, children engage in more complex forms of pretend play. Pretend play peaks at preschool age (three- to five-year-olds).[4, 5]

At early preschool age, children pretend with *invisible objects*. Now, you can host a tea party and drink invisible tea or eat a yummy invisible ice-cream cone.[1,6] These children will soon also engage in *enactment play*. This is when they imitate situations they have seen in their everyday lives.[7] For example, a three-year-old enjoys dressing up as mummy or daddy, cooking in their miniature kitchen, and vacuuming with their fake hoover. A similar form of pretend play is *replica play*. Here, children act out these situations

Table 4.1 Different forms of pretend play

Form of pretend play	*What is it?*	*Example*
Object substitution	A child pretends an object has a different function than it normally has.	Pretending a banana is a telephone.
Invisible object play	A child pretends they see an object that is not really there.	Taking a bite out of an invisible burger.
Enactment play	A child imitates situations they see in real life in play.	Hovering the living room with a fake vacuum cleaner.
Replica play	A child imitates situations they see in real life while playing with dolls or figurines.	Letting your doll hover the doll house living room.
Imaginary companions	A child pretends they have a friend who is invisible to others, or a toy or stuffed animal is their friend.	Hosting a tea party with Mr. Snuffles, the stuffed teddy, as your guest.
Impersonated characters play	A child pretends they are someone else.	Mom, I am not Emma. I am the Queen of England!
Paracosms	A child pretends they are living in an imaginary world with multiple pretend elements and rules. The child revisits the same imaginative play again and again.	Billy and Johnny, two brothers, like to go to "Magic world" when playing together. They make up interesting adventures. Last time, they fought off a dragon, and today they are back to see if there are any more dragons to fight off in order to find the pot of gold hidden in the cave in the backyard.

with dolls. About one in three children comes up with *imaginary companions*: they enjoy playing with their invisible friend for a long time.[8] These imaginary friends can exist in their imaginations for some weeks, and sometimes even years! Some children might not come up with a "fake friend" altogether but imagine a toy or a stuffed animal is their friend.

Furthermore, some kids pretend they themselves are someone else for an extended period of time. This is called *impersonated characters play*.[9] And to take the cake, some children create entirely imaginary worlds called *paracosms*. These worlds have many pretend elements and have their own imaginary rules.[10] In sum, *enactment play* (pretending to be mummy) and *replica play* (pretending your doll is a mummy) are clear forms of imitation. More importantly, you should buy that superhero costume when your kid is three to four years old!

WHY DO CHILDREN ENGAGE IN PRETEND PLAY?

Some might think play is a waste of time. After all, in the time a six-year-old pretends he is a superhero with laser-beam eyes, he could also have learned how to read and write, right? But developmental psychologists think otherwise. Studies show that play is actually crucial for development. In fact, it is *how* children learn. And pretend play is no different. Pretend play has been related to both cognitive skills and social skills, in other words, the learning motive and social motive of imitation described in Chapter 2 where we described theories of imitation.

CREATIVITY AND MATH

Cognitive skills relate to mental abilities to acquire knowledge, store information, and use this information. Many skills fall under this category: remembering things, doing maths, learning a new language, reasoning logically, and so on. The first cognitive skill that pretend play is related to is *creativity*.[11, 12] The more imaginative children are in their pretend play, the more creative they seem to be. One study followed schoolgirls over a four-year period.[13]

Figure 4.2 Children engaging in pretend play imitating their favorite superheroes!
Source: shutterstock.com.

Not only did they look at pretend play and creativity, but they also looked at how well these kids performed at school in *maths* (a second cognitive skill).

Again, children whose pretend play was more imaginative (and organized) were more creative. Children who showed enjoyment during pretend play came up with more original ideas too. Furthermore, pretend play and creativity both predicted the girls' math achievements four years later. The more imaginative the pretend play, and the more the girls enjoyed it, the better they performed at maths. Why is this? Perhaps in pretend play children practice with concepts such as symbolism (the idea that things can represent other things) and experimentation (trying things out), which are also useful in maths (Figure 4.2).

LANGUAGE

A third cognitive skill that is related to pretend play is *language*.[14, 15, 16] Language is quite interesting. Words are symbolic: they refer to things in the real world, but they do not necessarily share any features with them. Why, for example, is a "cup" named a cup? What about the word "cup" makes it inherently related to the object cup? A cup does not make a cuplike sound. Yet, still, if I would say "grab me a cup please", you know exactly what to do. And, you also know that I would not be too happy if you handed me a wine glass (similar in use, but clearly a different object) or a lion cub (similar in sound, yet very different from a cup). Hence, words refer to real-life objects, merely because we all agreed they do. Pretend play may be the perfect way for children to experiment with symbolic reasoning. A two-year-old holding a banana as a phone is practicing the symbolic meaning attached to an object and bending its meaning for fun. Some studies indeed showed that language skills go hand in hand with symbolic play in toddlers.[17, 18, 19]

COUNTERFACTUAL REASONING

A fourth cognitive skill that is strongly related to pretend play is *counterfactual reasoning*. This is just a fancy way of thinking about "What if something else were true?".[20, 21, 22] Children, generally, are really bad at applying this type of reasoning. If you would ask a four-year-old "What if all horses barked. Daisy is a horse. Does Daisy bark?", most likely they would say "No!". See, four-year-olds have much trouble letting go of their real-world knowledge. And in the real world, horses do *not* bark. Yet, in their play, children seem to be able to let go of their real-world knowledge and with ease can claim "I am a doggy, woof!". Pretend play can be thought of as crucial to learn hypothetical reasoning. It might just be the training ground for future scientists!

SOCIAL SKILLS

Pretend play is also important to foster *social skills*. First, children can try out *social roles* from the adult world.[23] According to famous psychologist Vygotsky (1896–1934), pretend play provides a safe arena where children can experiment with social situations and complicated emotions without the real-world consequences.[24] It is completely safe to try the role of a bossy teacher in pretend play. But in real life, being too bossy is often not appreciated by your friends. Interestingly, children with autism spectrum disorder engage less in pretend play. This might be one of the reasons for their troubles with social interactions.[25, 26, 27] However, it might also be the other way around: *because* these children have difficulties with social interactions, they do not enjoy pretend play as much and simply choose not to engage in it.

EMOTION REGULATION

Pretend play enhances *emotion regulation*, a second social skill. This is the ability to manage your emotions and to engage adaptively within your social environment.[12] Children are not very good at this at first: it is perfectly normal for a two-year-old to lay down on the floor screaming because they are not allowed to try and drink the dish soap. Children have to learn the cultural display rules of emotions: which emotions are okay to share and which should be hidden? Pretend play allows children to try and act out emotional experiences. As such, they can build their emotion regulation skills.[28, 29] Indeed, studies find that children who engage in pretend play are better at regulating their own emotions.[12]

THEORY OF MIND

The third and final social skill that is related to pretend play is *theory of mind*.[30,31] Theory of mind can be thought of as the art of "mind reading". Children before the age of four have not mastered this skill yet. They simply think that everyone knows, sees, and experiences exactly the same as they do. This is thought of as the reason why young children cannot lie and why they play hide-and-seek by merely closing their eyes. Around the age of four, children learn the theory of mind: they understand that someone else might have a different perspective than they do. Pretend play might help children learn this mind reading skill.

Take, for example, the game of "playing house". First, the roles have to be determined: who will play the daddy, who will play the baby, and, most importantly, who will play the doggy? This agreement is quite important because if roles are not clearly determined, things get confusing really quickly. The doggy biting the daddy in play is funny. George biting Billy in real life is not. Hence, in order to even *make the rules* of the play, children have to understand what information they need to convey. Does Billy know I am pretending to be a doggy? How will Billy react if I bite him? Without theory of mind, George (the doggy) might assume wrongly that it is clear to everyone else that he is now a doggy and that biting is funny doggy behavior. With the mindreading skill, George knows others cannot *know* he is pretending to be a doggy unless he tells them.

In the previous paragraph, we've described the role of imitation in childhood play. Specifically, we've described the various forms of pretend play and what skills potentially benefit from this kind of play. You may wonder why we just don't close all schools. If pretend play has so many advantages, why would we still need schooling? But see Box 4.1 for a critical note on that. In the next paragraph, we will further dive into imitation in childhood. We will discuss *why* children imitate and *who* they are likely to copy.

BOX 4.1 CRITICAL NOTE: THE CHICKEN OR THE EGG?

After reading the above about pretend play, you might conclude we should close schools, stop learning, and start playing more. Well, we don't blame you. Nowadays, in many parts of the world, children spend more and more time in school and extracurricular activities, and less and less time playing. However, before you decide to call your local elementary school to tell them you read a book on imitation and the importance of pretend play, please consider the following study.

A review study (a study in which lots of previously conducted studies are compared to each other) on pretend play aimed to find out if pretend play actually *causes* all these wonderful skills such as language, creativity, and reasoning to develop better. Or, on the other hand, that pretend play does not cause these skills to develop better.[18] In this second scenario, a child can spend hours pretending to be a superhero, but this does *not actually increase* their creativity. It just happens to be that children who are already very creative enjoy these types of play more.

Numerous skills were investigated in the review study, among others: language skills, dealing with emotions, social skills, reasoning, problem-solving, and creativity. There was *no support for causality*. Thus, we simply do not know for sure if spending more time pretend playing increases, for example, one's creativity. Hence, it's a chicken-or-the-egg story: we do not know for sure which comes first: pretend play (the chicken) or these skills (the eggs).

SIMON SAYS...

One of the authors' favorite childhood games was "Simon says". The pretence of the game is simple. The leader says "Simon says..." followed by a command such as "jump!", and all the followers then must execute the command. However, be aware, the leader might mislead you by saying the command without "Simon says...". In this case, you must ignore the command altogether. As a kid, I thought this was the most thrilling game, and my father was a professional at building up the tension and excitement in between commands.

SIMON SAYS IN REAL LIFE

The game Simon Says is clearly built on imitation, alongside other skills such as inhibition (the ability to *not* act out a command) and attention (listen carefully to the leader). This game is a beautiful metaphor for how children learn in real life. For a great deal, children learn by copying others.

Albert Bandura (1925–2021) was a very influential psychologist, best known for the *social learning theory*, often also referred to as *model learning* (see also Chapter 2). Names aside, Bandura was the first to state that children can learn by merely *watching others*.[32] For example, the boy in Figure 4.3 would have learned the aggressive behavior by watching someone else spanking a teddy. To prove this, Bandura came up with the Bobo doll study.[33] Children would watch an adult interact with a Bobo doll – a large inflatable doll-like figure. Half the children watched an adult act aggressively toward the Bobo doll: hitting and punching the doll, whilst saying things like "Kick him". The others watched an adult interact nicely with the doll, not behaving aggressively at all. Subsequently, the children were allowed to play with the Bobo doll themselves. You've probably guessed it: children watching an adult play aggressively copied their behaviors. They too yelled at the Bobo doll, kicked it, and punched it. Children who did not see this behavior did so very rarely. Hence, the saying "Do as I say, not as I do" might not cut it. Parenting really is leading by example.

Figure 4.3 A child copying aggressive behavior?
Source: shutterstock.com.

WHO DO CHILDREN IMITATE?

Children do not merely copy everyone they encounter. It makes sense that children are perhaps most likely to copy ones close to them (e.g., parents and siblings).[34] But children also copy (some) strangers. Children tend to copy *warm and friendly* strangers more than strangers acting aloof or antisocial.

One study tested this with very young children: 12-, 18-, and 24-month-olds.[35] The children watched a stranger open a box to retrieve a toy. Half the children watched the complete stranger, who ignored them mostly during the task. When the child entered the room with their parent, this stranger was reading in a corner. And when opening the box, the stranger did not make eye contact with the infant. The other half watched a very social stranger: before opening the box, the stranger played with them. And whilst opening the box, the stranger talked to them and made eye contact. Interestingly, the 12-month-olds did not really seem to care much: they copied the actions of both types of models to open the box. The 18-month-olds copied the outcome (successfully opening the box) when the stranger acted aloof. But when the stranger acted socially, they would copy *all* of the strangers' behaviors, even those not really relevant for opening the box! The 24-month-olds also copied the stranger, and they were less likely to successfully open the box when the stranger acted nonsocially. Apparently, these two-year-olds needed the social reinforcement as a motivation to open the box themselves.

Next to friendliness, children also look for other cues to know who to copy. One of those cues is how *similar* the model is to them in terms of group membership. In psychological literature, this is often called the *in-group* (versus the *out-group*). People have numerous in-groups: the family one belongs to, one's nationality, the soccer team one supports, or one's cultural background. If, for example, I identify as a Catholic New Yorker with an Italian background, who is a super fan of the Yankees, some of my in-groups might be Americans, Catholics, New Yorkers, Italians, and Yankees fans. My out-groups might be non-Americans, non-Catholics, people living in Texas, Dutch people, and Red Sox supporters.

Young children have in-groups and out-groups too. For example, for a child growing up in Englishspeaking surroundings, those who speak English are part of the in-group. Conversely, those who speak a foreign language can be thought of as the out-group.

One study tested this with four-to-five-year-olds.[36] First, children were introduced to two demonstrators: a native-speaker female and a female with a foreign accent. Then, the children were shown a picture of a novel object (e.g., a toilet plunger) and asked if they knew what the object was used for. They were asked who they thought could help them best: the native speaker or the nonnative speaker. Then, they watched both presenters show them how the object is used. Half the times, the native speaker showed the correct way, and the nonnative speaker a wrong usage. And for the other half this was the other way around. Lastly, children were asked to say which presenter performed the correct demonstration. The results might be a bit disturbing. These young children said they would like to ask the native speaker for help. In addition, they thought the native speakers were showing the correct use (regardless if they actually did). Thus, children tend to trust their in-group more for reliable information than an out-group.

Another study used a similar approach: four-to-five-year-olds watched two adults retrieve a toy from a special box.[37] One adult acted purely goal-oriented: all of his behaviors were necessary to open the box. The other also opened the box successfully but performed silly unnecessary behaviors (such as tapping the box three times on its side). Thereafter, one of the adults left the room, whilst the other gave the child the box to retrieve the toy themselves. Children tended to *copy the adult who was left in the room*. If the goal-oriented adult remained in the room, the children opened the box following all the necessary steps. But, if the other adult remained in the room, the children also copied their silly unnecessary steps. Thus, whoever is present is more likely to be copied.

Children also use information they have about the *previous performances* of their models. People who have shown in the past to be reliable are more likely to be imitated than those who have proven to be unreliable.[38] Take, for example, this study: 14-month-olds watched an adult act with familiar objects such as a pair of shoes. One adult acted reliably by putting the shoes on their feet. The other adult acted silly: putting the shoes on their hands. Next, children watched the adult interact in a novel way on an object (e.g., turning on a light with your forehead). Children's imitation of the adult's novel action (turning on the light using their own forehead) was influenced by the adult's reliability. If the adult put their shoes on the normal way – on their feet – the child was more likely to copy the adult, than if the adult had put their shoes on their hands.

Lastly, children also tend to copy *other* children. Similar to looking for cues about a model's previous performances, children look for cues about their peers to decide who to copy. One such cue is *age*. Children tend to copy *slightly older* children.[39] This is a smart tactic, as it is likely that with increasing age, people have more skills and knowledge than you do.

In fact, there are education systems that play into this. *Montessori* education deliberately groups children from different ages together so that they can learn from each other, for example, into two (three-to-six- and six-to-twelve-year-olds) or in three age groups (four-to-six-, six-to-nine-, and nine-to-twelve-year-olds).[40, 41] This way, children can experience what it is like to be the youngest and learn by imitating their older classmates. They will also learn what it is like to be the oldest, being the one copied.

A final cue children look for is *status*.[39] Popular kids are more likely to be imitated than unpopular kids. Of course, the same holds true for adults. In Chapter 2, we described the *prestige bias* explaining why adult women in the 1990s wanted to look like Rachel from *Friends*.

In the last paragraph, we have described *why* and *who* children imitate. Next, we will describe an advanced cognitive skill related to imitation in more depth: *theory of mind*. As indicated previously, this is often called the "mind reading skill" and develops in early childhood.

HIDE-AND-SEEK: WHY DO CHILDREN HIDE IN PLAIN SIGHT?

Playing hide-and-seek with a two-year-old guarantees for some fun. For adults, that is. Chances are, as you are slowly counting to ten, the little one runs to the nearest by curtains to effectively hide their face, but oddly forgets about the rest of their body. Or even better: the child closes their eyes and assumes the power of invisibility has descended over them. You spent the next couple of minutes pretending to have a hard time finding the child hiding in plain sight.

Hide-and-seek highlights how beautifully complex adult thinking really is. It is actually quite an advanced game, and two-year-olds are clearly not advanced enough to play it well. They do not seem to have the basic understanding that others can see, think, or know things, you yourself do not. Consequently, they wrongfully think "If I cannot see you, then you cannot see me either". At what age do children get better at this? And what does it have to do with imitation?

I KNOW WHAT YOU KNOW: THE SALLY-ANNE TASK

Children hiding in plain sight lack the understanding that they themselves know, think, and see things differently to others. In scientific studies, this skill is often tested with a *false belief task*. This refers to the idea that people act upon their beliefs, even if these are not in line with reality. If you left your car keys on the kitchen counter, this is the place you will look for them when you want to go out, even if your wife moved the keys to her purse. Hence, your belief ("the keys are on the counter") is not in line with reality ("the keys are in her purse"), and this is called a "false belief". You will act on your belief, not on the reality that you are unaware of.

The Sally-Anne task is a false belief task to test children's mind-reading skills.[42] In this task, Sally (typically a doll or hand puppet) places a marble in a basket and then leaves the room. Another character, Anne, enters and moves the marble to a box. Sally returns, and the child is asked "Where will Sally look for her marble?". The correct answer to this question would be "in the basket where she left it", as Sally is unaware Anne moved her marble. A child will only answer this question correctly if (s)he knows Sally will act upon her false belief ("the marble is in the basket") and not on the actual state of affairs ("Anne moved the marble to the box"). Children typically master this task at around four years old.[34]

This task is said to measure *theory of mind*, as children need to know what others know (in this case, Sally) in order to answer the question correctly. This is the exact same skill needed to play hide and seek. A child must be a good mind reader to know how to effectively hide themselves. "If I cannot see you, you cannot see me" does not cut it. The child must know that "mommy can see me, even if I cannot see her. But mommy cannot see through the couch. So, this is a good hiding spot. I should also hide my feet, otherwise mommy can spot me right away!".

CONGRATS, YOUR CHILD TOLD A LIE!

Most parents would not be too happy with their children lying to them. We generally consider it bad behaviour. However, we are here to tell you to celebrate the first time your child tells a lie! It is a big accomplishment and a clear sign they are developing into more complex beings. You can worry about them becoming polite beings later.

A two-year-old will gladly say "wow grandma, you look extra wrinkly today", but a seven-your-old will (probably) know better and lie. Also, most two-year-olds will likely honestly tell you they pooped their pants if you ask them, while most four-year-olds will try to hide this from you.

One experiment you can do at home is the *mean monkey experiment*. It goes like this: a child is presented with three stickers. Two boring looking stickers, and a special sparkly one. Clearly, everyone would prefer the *special* sticker over one of the boring ones. The experimenter holds a hand puppet resembling a monkey. The experimenter introduces the monkey to the child "This is mean monkey. He takes whatever sticker you like best. You will get to pick one of the stickers that is left". Thereafter, the child is asked to point to his or her favourite sticker. Following this, mean monkey takes this sticker and the experimenter says "You may now take one of the two stickers that are left". Think about a young child in your life, around the age of three or four. What do you think this kid would do?

If the child is about four years old, she or he is likely to have figured out how to lie. Maybe the first time meeting mean monkey they would honestly tell the monkey they like the sparkly sticker best. But, if they are asked to play a second round, they catch on and point to a boring sticker, claiming they think that one is the best sticker. This way, mean monkey takes the boring sticker and they can sneakily grab the sparkly sticker they liked all along. However, younger children, aged three and under, have not mastered the skill of lying yet. Over and over again, they will tell mean monkey they like the special sticker the most, only to be disappointed each time the monkey steals their sticker.

What does this tell us? Well, first of all, young children (aged three and under) are bad liars. But why is this the case? It likely has to do with the development of *theory of mind* which we also mentioned in Chapter 3 (imitation in infancy). Under the age of four, children simply cannot fathom the fact that they might have different thoughts and knowledge than others. There is no point to lying, if you think the mean monkey already knows the sparkly sticker is the one you fancy. And these young children might also wrongfully expect others think the same as they do. If they like the colour pink best, this simply *is* the most beautiful colour. Other opinions simply are not possible. Have you ever tried arguing with a two-year-old? You will lose!

Most children will learn *theory of mind* around the age of four. However, some might master this skill a bit earlier. Bilinguals for example tend to master the Sally-Anne task a few months earlier than monolinguals.[43] This is likely because bilingual children have more experience in reading minds. From the start, these children need to know what others know ("What language does grandma speak? English or Spanish?") in order to know how to respond to a question ("Yes" or "Sí"). Other children might have a disadvantage: they learn the mindreading skill at a later age. And some continue to have troubles with this for the rest of their lives. This is a symptom often found in children and adults with autism spectrum disorder.[29]

THE MINDREADING SKILL AND IMITATION

You might wonder what theory of mind has to do with imitation. First, it is important to note that the relation between imitation and theory of mind is not clear-cut. That is, different psychologists might think differently about this. There is a reason to believe that different social skills are intertwined: the same parts of the brain are thought to be active when performing these tasks. One interesting review paper (a paper summarizing a bunch of earlier conducted studies) asserts three things.[44] First, imitation seems innate to humans as very young infants might already imitate others (but remember from Chapter 3 that this idea is challenged by later studies on infant imitation!). The review also describes evidence from neuroscience, including the existence of mirror neurons, suggesting this as well (see Chapter 2).

Second, imitation precedes theory of mind in development (*children can imitate before they develop theory of mind*) and in evolution (*simpler beings can imitate, but only complex beings can read minds*). Third and most importantly, imitation provides the (neural) mechanism by which theory of mind and empathy develop.[43] Simply put, it means that being a skilled imitator is necessary to becoming a skilled mind reader. Or at the very least: it helps one become a mind reader.

However, the importance of imitation for theory of mind skills might be challenged by findings from studies with people with autism spectrum disorder. Many people diagnosed with autism spectrum disorder have difficulties with theory of mind, and children with autism often show different behaviors in their play.[45] They, for example, show less interaction with peers and show less symbolic play (as-if play) and less qualitative pretend play.[46, 47] However, studies show mixed results when it comes to imitational behaviors of children with autism spectrum disorder. Some find that children with autism spectrum disorder show *less* imitation, whilst other studies find *no difference* in comparison with other children at all.[48, 49]

So, what should you take away from this? That the relation between *imitation* and *theory of mind* is under debate. Some scholars think they are similar and perhaps depend on each other (in order to learn how to mindread, one must first learn how to imitate). However, others argue they are not really that related at all. In the end, scientists are just like normal people, and sometimes disagree with each other!

In this paragraph, *theory of mind* development and the relation to imitation have been described. Next, we will look into the concept of the *zone of proximal development (ZPD).* This concept hovers somewhere in between instruction and imitation: the tasks a child can do with a little help from someone more advanced.

WITH A LITTLE BIT OF HELP ... I CAN DO ANYTHING!

Children do not only learn by literally copying their parents but also learn in other ways. For example, they can learn by instruction: "No Johnny! Jumping off that wall would make you break your leg. Don't do that". Or by experiencing the natural *consequences* themselves: "Apparently when I go outside without shoes on, my feet get cold". And sometimes by experiencing the "*consequences*" imposed on them via parenting: "Johnny stop hitting your sister, or else… no telly for you tonight!". There is one form of learning that hovers in between instruction and imitation: learning from others by *doing it together.*

At any stage of life, there are things we are well capable to do on our own, things we simply cannot do at all, and things we are only able to do with a little help from someone else. In fact, reading this might made you think of one of those skills for yourself.

Children also learn various skills by doing it *together* with someone more skilled, such as a parent or an older sibling. The previously mentioned psychologist Vygotsky is well known for his theory called the *zone of proximal development (ZPD)*. By definition, this is the difference between what a child can do by itself and what a child can do under the guidance of an adult or more capable peers.[29] Four-year-olds generally cannot make a 1,000-piece jigsaw puzzle all by themselves. It is much too difficult. But, together with an older sibling, they can. Thus, this specific 1,000-piece jigsaw is within the ZPD of four-year-olds. In this zone is where children learn new skills best according to Vygotsky, for example, by closely watching the older siblings' puzzle-solving techniques and making them their own.

This ties back to Montessori education described earlier. Here, children are deliberately grouped together with children of different ages and corresponding skill levels. Hence, this type of classroom creates many opportunities for children to learn in their ZPD. When cooperating with an older, more advanced classmate, the younger child can learn new skills.

Next, we will look at language learning in childhood. As always, we will look at language learning through the lens of imitation.

LANGUAGE LEARNING: THE EPITOME OF IMITATION?

One of the most wondrous things to witness is a child's language development. It seems to start out of nowhere, often with a simple "dada" or "mama". But before you know it, the child's vocabulary expands ("ball", "cat", "RAAWR"), incorporates simple grammar ("dada ball", "look cat", "dino RAAWR"), and later on is comparable to that of an adult ("look mommy, the cat plays with the ball!").

It is truly amazing when you think about the fact that there are over 6,900 different languages in the world, each with their own words, grammar rules, and dialects.[50] Some are more similar to each other (such as French to Spanish or Dutch to German) than others (English to Mandarin). Yet … all over the world children seem to learn their mother tongues with ease. It seems to happen without any effort. At least, much less effort than it would take an adult to learn a new language from scratch. Have you ever tried to do so? Even if we put in lots of hours studying the language, we will likely never be as good as a native speaker. One of the most difficult things to capture is the correct pronunciation of a new language: a thick accent will always give us away. This begs the question: *how do children learn language?*

In this paragraph, we first describe a great debate amongst philosophers: is language an acquired skill or are humans born with innate knowledge about language? Next, we will describe shortly how the typical language development in children looks like. At what age do children master various language skills? Lastly, we will come back to the overarching question: what role does imitation play?

ARE CHILDREN INNATE LANGUAGE EXPERTS?

What do you think? Are children born as blank slates, knowing nothing about the world, and able to learn whatever you expose them to (beautifully called *tabula rasa* in Latin)? Or is everything already inside us, predestined by our genes? This is the central question of the *nature–nurture debate.* Scientists have argued for centuries if everything humans know is learned (nurture) or predestined (nature) (see also Chapter 3 on the discussion about whether imitation itself is innate or learned).

Those in favor of the *tabula rasa* argument are in good company. The ancient Greek philosopher Aristotle was the first to formulate this idea. In the 17th century, he was joined by the English philosopher John Locke. Thinking all children are born as blank slates would mean that everything you know is learned during your life, including language. This, one could claim, is why we don't all speak Mandarin, German, and Spanish. You cannot speak a language you have never been exposed to.

Not to worry, those against the *tabula rasa* argument are not in bad company either. The Greek philosopher Plato is your friend: he thought humans have immortal souls, bringing whatever learned in a previous life with us to the next. But also philosophers such as Descartes and Spinoza agree with you. These philosophers would argue people are not blank slates at all. The extreme end of this view would be that nothing is learned, and everything is predestined. The discovery of genes backs this claim up: people are born with information *inside* them. This is why all people are able to learn language: somewhere inside us is the innate "knowledge" about what to do with the stream of sounds thrown at us from a young age. Thus, one could claim babies are in fact able to learn language, because they are *not* blank slates.

Most of these great thinkers are long gone. But one thinker important for the nature–nurture debate on language is still alive: Noam Chomsky. Chomsky is a famous American linguist, philosopher, and political activist, born in 1928. He is one of the most influential language scientists from the 20th century. He formulated an important idea: the hypothesis of *universal grammar.* Chomsky claimed that language is innate to humans. This can explain why different languages have so many similarities. In the 1960s, Chomsky even claimed humans all have a "language acquisition device" (LAD) – an instinctive mental capacity enabling infants to acquire and produce language. Chomsky figured it should be somewhere in the brain. Similar to how the lungs are needed for breathing, the LAD is needed for language. Chomsky reasoned that children should have some sort of language device: how else would they be able to learn language with such ease and without clear instructions?

You might wonder who is right: who won the debate? Are our brains blank slates at birth, or are we born with preexisting knowledge? We are sorry to tell you, but the result is a boring draw. Both won and both lost. With the help of modern scientific techniques, we know pretty sure there is no special organ in your brain dedicated to language. However, we do know that there are areas of the brain that are active when you produce language, namely Broca's area. And that other areas of the brain are required to understand the meaning of language, namely Wernicke's area.[51] Furthermore, we know that people are not entirely blank slates: our genes hold valuable information affecting our appearances, thoughts, and behaviors. Thus, we are *not* blank slates. However, we also know that in order to learn language, children have to be exposed to it: one's surroundings do play an important role (and one of those roles is likely played by imitation). Tragic stories such as that of a girl called Genie described in Box 4.2 tell us that when children are not exposed to language in childhood, they will not be able to fully learn it later on.

BOX 4.2 THE STORY OF GENIE

In the 1970s in Los Angeles, a 13-year-old girl was discovered. The girl was later named Genie to remain her confidentiality. The story of Genie is very tragic. When she was discovered, she did not look like the average 13-year-old. She is described as looking like a seven-year-old, being short and weighing only about 26 kilograms. This was the result of years of horrible abuse imposed on her by her parents. Genie was kept in a room, away from the outside world. She was tied to a potty by day and tied to her bed by night. She had not learned how to walk and talk. Upon discovery, Genie was barely able to communicate verbally at all. She had never interacted with other humans.

As tragic as Genie's story is, it is also a very important story for scientists. Namely, after being removed from her parents, Genie's development was closely studied. First, Genie seemed to develop quickly. She became a happy, playful girl. Importantly, she started to learn language. First, she learned words, and soon she mastered two-word sentences. But, sadly, Genie never fully mastered language. Her language remained at the level of a two-and-a-half-year-old. For linguists, Genie's story underscored the idea of a *critical period for language*: humans have to be exposed to language in their childhood, in order to learn it properly. Scientists concluded that single words can be acquired later in life, but the rules of word order in language cannot.

HOW DO CHILDREN LEARN LANGUAGE?

Moving away from the debate, we still need to answer the question: how do children learn language? And, more specifically, what does imitation have to do with it?

Let's first consider the stages in which children learn language. All children progress through these stages in the same order but at slightly different rates. Two-month-old children make *cooing* sounds. What is fascinating is that these noises are the same for babies across the globe! Thus, an Indian baby makes the same typical baby sound as a Chinese baby. Six-month-old children start *babbling*. Babbling is different from cooing: it is comprised of a string of syllables ("dadada"). At first, the babbles do not really seem to resemble the language the child grows up in. It perhaps is merely a good practice for their vocal tracts. Gradually, the babbles become more attuned to the language. Specifically, the intonation patterns will be typical to the surrounding language. Hence, these infants *copy* the sounds and melodies from the languages they hear. Native Hindi speakers will be able to identify a Hindi-speaking baby merely by listening to the baby. Similarly, a Chinese speaker can identify a Chinese babbling baby.

Somewhere between 10–20 months, children utter their very first word. Hooray! Generally speaking, girls do so earlier than boys. This is called the *one-word stage*. Slowly, children will learn more and more words (dada, ball, bird) but lack grammatical words (might, to, is). In Table 4.2, we present a list of first words that children in different parts of the world speak.

Between 18–24 months, children enter the *two-word stage*. These children make short sentences (daddy hat, want apple, me spoon). Interestingly, these two-word sentences already reflect the grammar rules of the language. Children say "gimme hat" and not "hat gimme". But children still lack purely grammar words (might, to, is). At the same time (18–24-months), children rapidly expand their vocabulary. The two-word stage lasts for several months. Soon thereafter, children can make much longer sentences; even more than 10 words in one sentence are now possible. In these longer sentences, children also use grammar words.

At around two to three years old, children learn the vast majority of grammar. By the age of five, the average child knows about

Table 4.2 The first ten words children produce in four different languages (translated to English)[52]

	English (American)	*French*	*Korean*	*Turkish*
1	Mommy	Daddy	Mommy	Mommy
2	Daddy	Mommy	Daddy	Yum yum
3	Ball	Baby	Peekaboo	Brother
4	Bye	Bye	Woof woof	Woof woof
5	Hi	Thank you	Cracker	Baby
6	No	Bread	Water	Vroom
7	Dog	Peekaboo	Baby	Bye
8	Baby	Ball	Yes	Water
9	Woof woof	Sock	Ball	Ball
10	Banana	Shoe	No	Doll

10,000 words and mastered practically all grammar. They make mistakes sometimes (e.g., two mens), but other than that they have little language left to learn.

IT ALL BEGINS WITH LISTENING

Un ver vert verse un verre vers un verrier vers vingt heures is a perfectly normal French sentence that translates into "A green worm pours a glass towards a glassmaker around eight o'clock". We urge you to let a French native speaker (or Google Translate) read this sentence aloud to you. Chances are you will hear "vèr vèr vèr vèr vèr vèr vèr", not being able to pick up the slight differences in pronunciations a native speaker would. Why is this the case?

Unless you have been exposed to a language, you are unable to pick up all the sounds, and often also have difficulty producing them. The harsh "ghh" sound in Dutch is very difficult for non-Dutch speakers to produce. Similarly, many Chinese struggle with the "R/L" sound. If a foreign language uses sounds your native language does not, your brain will not learn to differentiate them. Hence, you end up hearing "vèr vèr vèr vèr vèr vèr vèr" and not "Un ver vert verse un verre vers un verrier vers vignt heure".

Interestingly, very young infants are *better* at this than you are. At birth, people are able to differentiate sounds from *all languages*. Infants aged six to eight months can differentiate between sounds used in all languages equally well. But slightly older babies, aged 10–12 months, lose this superpower: they start to realign with their native language. Interestingly, bilingual babies will learn to discriminate the sounds of *both* languages at 10–12 months.[53, 54]

So, what does this tell us? At first, our brains are equally good (or equally bad) at differentiating sounds from *all languages*. A baby born in Finland has an equally good chance at mastering Mandarin as a baby born in China. But at around 10–12 months, just when most children start to utter their very first word, babies lose this skill. Our brains become wired to the language(s) we are exposed to. Hence, our brains prepare us to learn all the sounds, words, and language rules of the language(s) we've heard since birth. Ready to copy them and make them our own.

IMITATION AND LANGUAGE

Thus far, you've read about the language development of babies (cooing, babbling, one-word sentences, two-word stage, many-word stage), and how humans at ten months already have become accustomed to their native language. But what does imitation have to do with all of this?

That's easy: learning language *is* imitation. Children are little copying machines. They copy every word and grammar from more advanced speakers around them. Scientific studies back this up. One study, for example, (with adults) showed that if people imitate an unfamiliar accent, they understand other sentences in this language better than participants who also listen to it but did not try to imitate it. Simply put, by imitating an accent you become better at understanding it too.[55]

Furthermore, brain scientists have discovered many interesting things about language learning. For example, the mirror system was first discovered in *area F5 in the frontal cortex* of monkeys, which in humans would be called *Broca's area* (the part of the brain active when producing language).[56] (See Chapter 2 for more details about the mirror neuron system.) Interestingly, brain imaging studies also show that the mirror system in the brain is active when people watch movements of the foot, hand, and mouth. But this is surprising: the mirror system is also activated when these people *read* phrases about these movements.[57] This is the important conclusion: the same brain mechanisms for imitation seem to play a role in language.[58]

In the previous paragraph, we have looked at the role of imitation in learning one's first language. Language learning seems to happen automatically without much effort. Children seem to be little sponges, absorbing words and grammar from their parents. Next, we look at the dark side of imitation, namely fear learning. Do children also copy their parents' fears?

DO FEARFUL PARENTS MAKE FEARFUL KIDS?

One in three people will have an anxiety disorder at some point in their life, meaning their everyday life is heavily impacted by excruciating fear.[59] Childhood and adolescence are the core risk periods for developing fear disorder.[60] Typically, the onset of one's first (or only) fear disorder is in childhood.[61, 62] These can take many specific forms, such as specific phobias including the fear of spiders, heights, clowns, or busy places. Some people experience more generalized fears. These fears are not related to a place or an object (e.g., people with generalized anxiety disorder or a panic disorder).

Many psychologists have tried to answer the question "why do people develop such fears?", and more specifically "do children learn these fears from their parents?".

WHAT DO GENETICS HAVE TO DO WITH IT?

Are fearful parents more likely to have fearful kids? Unfortunately, the answer is yes. Many studies have now shown evidence that children of parents with an anxiety disorder are more likely to develop such a disorder as well, in comparison with children of parents without these extreme fears.[63, 64] There are multiple explanations for this. Roughly, they fall into two categories: inherited and learned.

The first category has very little to do with imitational behaviors, but everything to do with the copying machine that is the human reproduction system: *genetics*. It isn't hard to imagine the basic traits such as hair color are inherited from our parents. We see it all the time: red-haired parents with freckles tend to have little red-haired freckled babies. But did you know we also inherit more complex traits such as the way we think and the way we act?

The science behind this is a bit tricky. After all, how do we know for sure that you inherited your bad temper from your easily frustrated father? Perhaps you did not inherit it through his genes but *learned* it by example? Watching your father cussing at a rude motorist, being overly annoyed when the milk soured, or yelling at a customer service employee through the phone ... is behaviour you can copy later on. Scientists have found clever ways to study this with by far the most interesting: twin and adoptee studies![65]

TWIN STUDIES AND ADOPTEE STUDIES: NATURE VERSUS NURTURE

Identical twins share their DNA. Genetically speaking, they *are the same person*. Exact copies through and through. And yet... Even though they might look the same, (over time) identical twins tend to differ. Perhaps one enjoys coffee, whilst the other thinks it's disgusting. One might play soccer every day of her life and become very good at it, whilst the other never touched a ball. Any differences between identical twins cannot be explained by their genetics: these are the exact same. Thus, any difference must be because they have had different *life experiences*. It is not *nature* (your genes) that causes these differences but *nurture* (your experiences).

Fraternal twins are interesting to study too. Genetically, they are no more the same (or different) than any two siblings. They just happen to be born at the same time. They are made up from two different egg cells and two different sperm cells. Comparing fraternal twins to identical twins yields very interesting and important scientific results. Let's say scientists want to find out if the preference for ice-cream flavors is inherited through our genes. They could ask hundreds of pairs of identical twins and fraternal twins this question: "What ice-cream flavor do you like best?". If the identical pairs more often agree (e.g., both liking chocolate) than the fraternal pairs, the researchers can conclude that genes affect preference for ice-cream flavor. Apparently, somewhere in the human genome, some information is stored about what flavors you like.

Another very informative way to study the effect of genes is by studying *adopted children*. These children grow up away from their biological parents. Thus, the effects of their surroundings are separated from the effects of their genes. Let's say the psychologists again want to find out if the preference for ice-cream flavor is inherited through our genes or learned behavior from our environment. They could ask this question "What ice-cream flavor do you like best?" to the biological parents, the adoptive parents, and the children.

This time, the researchers look for who the children are more in line with: do they like the same flavor as their biological parents or as their adoptive parents? If they have the same preference as their biological parents, whom they never met, it is very unlikely this is "learned" behavior. They probably inherited it through their genes. If they, as a group, have the same preferences as their adoptive parents, the scientists can conclude the preference for ice-cream flavor is learned.

For behaviors, it would be quite silly to say the exact behavior itself is predetermined by genetics. Nowhere in your DNA it is written that you will raise your arm at 7 am on January 2nd, open the cupboard, grab a cup, look for coffee in the cupboard, only to be very annoyed to find out you ran out of coffee, mumble some angry words at yourself, and write down *COFFEE* on your shopping list. However, you might be predisposed to *enjoy* bitter flavors (such as coffee), to be bad at planning, or to be easily annoyed and bad-tempered.

Back to anxiety disorders. Are these inherited through our genes or learned through behavior? Most likely, the answer is both. Twin studies typically find mild-to-moderate genetic influences on a variety of anxiety measures. These include self-reported anxiety symptoms, parent-reported symptoms, and clinically diagnosed disorders.[66] Furthermore, this relation is not limited to the specific type of fear.[67] For example, a parent terribly afraid of spiders might raise a child who is not afraid of spiders per se, but is troubled by a panic disorder. Hence, it is not the diagnosis per se that is transmitted in the genes but a proneness to becoming a fearful person.

However, this relation is not one-on-one. This means that, luckily, not all children of anxious parents become anxious themselves. It also means that not all anxious children were raised by fearful parents. Thus, there is some room for other influences: the environment one grows up in matters too!

WHAT DO WE KNOW ABOUT FEAR LEARNING?

There are various routes through which fear is transmitted from parent to child, other than genetics. For example, fearful parents are more likely to be overly protective of their children.[68] In the Netherlands, these parents are called "curling parents". This refers to how they try their best to smooth out the icy curling track of life for their youngsters. Others might call them "helicopter parents", hovering over their little ones, watching carefully so they can prevent any harm from happening. These parents have the very best intentions. They simply want their kids to have a pleasant, harmless life. However, an unintended side effect of bundling up your children in figurative bubble wrap is the message it conveys: "Be careful!", "It is a scary world", and "You are in danger!". Before you know it, children adopt these beliefs and the corresponding behaviors.

Another route through which fear can be transmitted is through *model learning*. As described in Chapter 2 (and earlier in this chapter), model learning is when you learn new behaviors or skills by observing others. Fear can be learned via this route as well. For example, in a famous experiment, rhesus monkeys *watched* other monkeys interact fearfully with snakes.[69] What happened? The on-watching monkeys became fearful of snakes themselves too. Interestingly, it is possible to teach rhesus monkeys to be afraid of flowers. However, this fear will *not* be copied by the on-watching monkeys. Apparently, rhesus monkeys have a "preparedness" for the fear of snakes (which indeed can be lethal) but not for flowers (which are typically harmless).

In humans, fear learning starts at a very early age. Take, for example, this study: mothers of toddlers were asked to act with either fear or happiness in regard to two toys: a rubber snake and a rubber spider.[70] The toddlers watched their moms react to the toys. Ten minutes later, the children were presented with the toys again. This time, the mothers were asked to keep a neutral facial expression. As you might expect, the children whose mothers reacted with fear also showed greater fear expressions when they saw the toys again.

You might have experienced the following yourself. Upon meeting a child for the first time, they might act a bit shy. Perhaps the child hides behind their parents' leg or tries to avoid eye contact at all costs. Soon however, as you keep chatting with the parent, the child relaxes and seems to enjoy your company. Is this learned behavior too? Probably, yes. One study, for example, showed that when mothers respond anxiously to a stranger, one-year-olds were also fearful and avoidant of this person. However, if mothers reacted nonanxiously, they were less likely to do so.[71]

In a study, children aged 6–17 years watched videos of one of their parents and a stranger whilst they were learning new fears.[72] The "fear learning" was done in a very common way for experimental studies. The adult is shown various shapes on a computer screen, and some are accompanied by an unpleasant loud noise. Over time, the adults learned which shapes (e.g., squares) were accompanied by the annoying noise and which weren't (e.g. circles).

Just imagine yourself doing this task. What face would you make when you would see the square popping up, knowing in a few seconds you will hear that annoying sound again? Probably an apprehensive, nasty looking face. The children watched the video of their parents, being able to see their faces, but were not exposed to the nasty sounds themselves. The children showed stronger fear learning when they observed their parent. This means that they too made nasty faces when being presented with the square and reported liking the squares less. Importantly, they did not show these imitation reactions when they watched a stranger. The researchers now knew one thing: apparently children learn fear more easily from their parents than from strangers!

One interesting aspect about this study is that the participants were put inside MRI scanners. These machines scan the activity in the brain, resulting in three-dimensional images of the participants' brain. This way, the researchers knew which areas in the brain were active during the task. Whilst watching their parents learning fear of shapes, the *amygdala* was active in the children's' brain. The amygdala is the part of the brain mainly responsible for emotions. Furthermore, researchers observed that there was an activity in the links between the amygdala and the *medial prefrontal cortex*. To summarize it very briefly, this is the front of your brain which is generally active when you make decisions, plan, and *mimic others*.

In sum, although children might be predisposed by their genetic baggage to be more (or less) fearful, they also learn fear by watching others. Parents might play a special role in this. This is because children watch their parents carefully for information about the world.

CONCLUSION

In this chapter, we have discussed some interesting topics of imitation in childhood. Children enjoy imitating others in their play (*pretend play*), which is a very effective way of learning about the world they grow up in. As children develop into more complex beings, they develop so-called *theory of mind* – the ability to think about the thoughts and motives of others. Making it perfectly possible to say, "I know, that you think my boots are beautiful, because Samantha told me, that you told her, that you are jealous of my new boots." Imitation is likely related to theory of mind: imitating others (in play) may facilitate learning this skill. We've discussed how children learn by imitating others, sometimes needing a helping hand along the way. Next, we've discussed that children are masters at learning a new language and that imitation helps them to do it. Lastly, we've discussed the "dark side" of imitation: children not only learn all the wonderful things their parents want them to but also copy their unwanted behavior. This is one of the reasons children with fearful parents are more likely to become fearful themselves too. To conclude, imitation helps children learn new skills and make sense of the world around them.

BOX 4.3 WHAT YOU SHOULD DEFINITELY REMEMBER FROM THIS CHAPTER

- Children show imitation in their play. This type of play is called pretend play. Pretend play is related to a bunch of cognitive skills such as creativity, language, and counterfactual reasoning. Pretend play is also related to social skills such as emotion regulation and theory of mind.
- Children tend to copy warm and friendly people. Furthermore, they tend to imitate others who are similar to them, are reliable based on previous performances, are older than them, or are popular.
- Children learn language across the globe in a similar way. At first, infants have the capacity to learn any language. However, at about 10–12 months, children attune to the language they grow up with. Language learning relies heavily on imitation.
- Children can learn fears through imitation as well. Unfortunately, fearful parents make fearful children.

NOTES

1 Weisberg, D. S. (2015). Pretend play. *Wiley Interdisciplinary Reviews: Cognitive Science*, *6*(3), 249–261. https://doi.org/10.1002/wcs.1341
2 Lillard, A. S. (1993). Pretend play skills and the child's theory of mind. *Child Development*, *64*(2), 348–371. https://doi.org/10.2307/1131255
3 Bosco, F. M., Friedman, O., & Leslie, A. M. (2006). Recognition of pretend and real actions in play by 1-and 2-year-olds: Early success and why they fail. *Cognitive Development*, *21*(1), 3–10. https://doi.org/10.1016/j.cogdev.2005.09.006

4 Lillard, A. S. (2017). Why do the children (pretend) play? *Trends in Cognitive Sciences, 21*(11), 826–834. https://doi.org/10.1016/j.tics.2017.08.001
5 Singer, D., & Singer, J. (1990). *Children's play and the developing imagination.* Cambridge, MA: Harvard University Press.
6 Taylor, M., & Carlson, S. M. (1997). The relation between individual differences in fantasy and theory of mind. *Child Development, 68*(3), 436–455. https://doi.org/10.1111/j.1467-8624.1997.tb01950.x
7 Lillard, A., Pinkham, A. M., & Smith, E. (2011). *Pretend play and cognitive development.* In U. Goswami (Ed.), *The Wiley-Blackwell handbook of childhood cognitive development* (pp. 285–311). New Jersey: Wiley-Blackwell.
8 Carter, C., & Bath, C. (2018). The pirate in the pump: Children's views of objects as imaginary friends at the start of school. *Education 3–13, 46*(3), 335–344. https://doi.org/10.1080/03004279.2016.1262887
9 Carlson, S. M., & Taylor, M. (2005). Imaginary companions and impersonated characters: Sex differences in children's fantasy play. *Merrill-Palmer Quarterly (1982-)*, 93–118. Retrieved from: https://www.jstor.org/stable/23096051
10 Taylor, M., Mottweiler, C. M., Aguiar, N. R., Naylor, E. R., & Levernier, J. G. (2020). Paracosms: The imaginary worlds of middle childhood. *Child Development, 91*(1), e164–e178. https://doi.org/10.1111/cdev.13162
11 Hoffmann, J., & Russ, S. (2012). Pretend play, creativity, and emotion regulation in children. *Psychology of Aesthetics, Creativity, and the Arts, 6*(2), 175. https://doi.org/10.1037/a0026299
12 Hoffmann, J. D., & Russ, S. W. (2016). Fostering pretend play skills and creativity in elementary school girls: A group play intervention. *Psychology of Aesthetics, Creativity, and the Arts, 10*(1), 114–125. https://doi.org/10.1037/aca0000039
13 Wallace, C. E., & Russ, S. W. (2015). Pretend play, divergent thinking, and math achievement in girls: A longitudinal study. *Psychology of Aesthetics, Creativity, and the Arts, 9*(3), 296–305. https://doi.org/10.1037/a0039006
14 Kim, S. (2018). *Pretend play and language development among preschool children: A meta-analysis* (Doctoral dissertation). Retrieved from: https://krex.k-state.edu/dspace/handle/2097/38859
15 Lillard, A. S., Lerner, M. D., Hopkins, E. J., Dore, R. A., Smith, E. D., & Palmquist, C. M. (2013). The impact of pretend play on children's development: A review of the evidence. *Psychological Bulletin, 139*(1), 1–34. https://doi.org/10.1037/a0029321
16 Weisberg, D. S. (2015). Pretend play. *Wiley Interdisciplinary Reviews: Cognitive Science, 6*(3), 249–261. https://doi.org/10.1002/wcs.1341

17 Bruner, J. (1985). Child's talk: Learning to use language. *Child Language Teaching and Therapy*, *1*(1), 111–114. https://doi.org/10.1177/026565908500100113
18 Quinn, S., Donnelly, S., & Kidd, E. (2018). The relationship between symbolic play and language acquisition: A meta-analytic review. *Developmental Review*, *49*, 121–135. https://doi.org/10.1016/j.dr.2018.05.005
19 Weisberg, D. S., & Gopnik, A. (2013). Pretense, counterfactuals, and Bayesian causal models: Why what is not real really matters. *Cognitive Science*, *37*(7), 1368–1381. https://doi.org/10.1111/cogs.12069
20 Gopnik, A., & Walker, C. M. (2013). Considering counterfactuals: The relationship between causal learning and pretend play. *American Journal of Play*, *6*(1), 15–28. Retrieved from: https://psycnet.apa.org/record/2014-22061-004
21 Murray, D. (2014). The philosophical baby: What children's minds tell us about truth, love, and the meaning of life, by Alison Gopnik. *Teaching Philosophy*, *37*(1), 118–122. https://doi.org/10.5840/teachphil20143719
22 Weisberg, D. S., & Gopnik, A. (2013). Pretense, counterfactuals, and Bayesian causal models: Why what is not real really matters. *Cognitive Science*, *37*(7), 1368–1381. https://doi.org/10.1111/cogs.12069
23 Bottema-Beutel, K., Kim, S. Y., & Crowley, S. (2019). A systematic review and meta-regression analysis of social functioning correlates in autism and typical development. *Autism Research*, *12*(2), 152–175. https://doi.org/10.1002/aur.2055
24 M. Cole, V. John-Steiner, S. Scribner, & E. Souberman, (1978, Eds.), *Mind in society: The development of higher mental processes. L.S. Vygotsky.* Cambridge, MA: Harvard University Press.
25 Campbell, S. B., Leezenbaum, N. B., Mahoney, A. S., Moore, E. L., & Brownell, C. A. (2016). Pretend play and social engagement in toddlers at high and low genetic risk for autism spectrum disorder. *Journal of Autism and Developmental Disorders*, *46*(7), 2305–2316. https://doi.org/10.1007/s10803-016-2764-y
26 Happé, F. (2015). Autism as a neurodevelopmental disorder of mind-reading. *Journal of the British Academy*, *3*, 197–209. https://doi.org/10.5871/jba/003.197
27 Brunsdon, V. E., & Happé, F. (2014). Exploring the 'fractionation'of autism at the cognitive level. *Autism*, *18*(1), 17–30. https://doi.org/10.1177/1362361313499456
28 Howes, C., & Matheson, C. C. (1992). Sequences in the development of competent play with peers: Social and social pretend play. *Developmental Psychology*, *28*, 961–974. https://doi.org/10.1037/0012-1649.28.5.961

29 Slot, P. L., Mulder, H., Verhagen, J., & Leseman, P. P. (2017). Preschoolers' cognitive and emotional self-regulation in pretend play: Relations with executive functions and quality of play. *Infant and Child Development, 26*(6), e2038. https://doi.org/10.1002/icd.2038
30 Wellman, H. M., Cross, D., & Watson, J. (2001). Meta-analysis of theory-of-mind development: The truth about false belief. *Child Development, 72*(3), 655–684. https://doi.org/10.1111/1467-8624.00304
31 Lin, S. K., Tsai, C. H., Li, H. J., Huang, C. Y., & Chen, K. L. (2017). Theory of mind predominantly associated with the quality, not quantity, of pretend play in children with autism spectrum disorder. *European Child & Adolescent Psychiatry, 26*(10), 1187–1196. https://doi.org/10.1007/s00787-017-0973-3
32 Bandura, A. (1989). Social cognitive theory. In R. Vasta (Ed.), *Annals of child development, Volume 6. Six Theories of Child Development*. Greenwich, CT: JAI Press.
33 Bandura, A., Ross, D., & Ross, S. A. (1961). Transmission of aggression through imitation of aggressive models. *The Journal of Abnormal and Social Psychology, 63*(3), 575–582. https://doi.org/10.1037/h0045925
34 Wilks, M., Kirby, J., & Nielsen, M. (2019). Developmental changes in young children's willingness to copy the antisocial actions of ingroup members in a minimal group context. *Developmental Psychology, 55*(4), 709–721. https://doi.org/10.1037/dev0000667
35 Nielsen, M. (2006). Copying actions and copying outcomes: Social learning through the second year. *Developmental Psychology, 42*(3), 555–565. https://doi.org/10.1037/0012-1649.42.3.555
36 Kinzler, K. D., Corriveau, K. H., & Harris, P. L. (2011). Children's selective trust in native-accented speakers. *Developmental Science, 14*(1), 106–111. https://doi.org/10.1111/j.1467-7687.2010.00965.x
37 Nielsen, M., & Blank, C. (2011). Imitation in young children: When who gets copied is more important than what gets copied. *Developmental Psychology*, 47(4), 1050–1053. https://doi.org/10.1037/a0023866
38 Zmyj, N., Buttelmann, D., Carpenter, M., & Daum, M. M. (2010). The reliability of a model influences 14-month-olds' imitation. *Journal of Experimental Child Psychology, 106*(4), 208–220. https://doi.org/10.1016/j.jecp.2010.03.002
39 Wood, L. A., Kendal, R. L., & Flynn, E. G. (2013). Whom do children copy? Model-based biases in social learning. *Developmental Review, 33*(4), 341–356. https://doi.org/10.1016/j.dr.2013.08.002
40 Lillard, A., & Else-Quest, N. (2006). The early years: Evaluating Montessori education. *Science, 313*(5795), 1893–1894. https://doi.org/10.1126/science.1132362
41 Derived from https://montessori.nl/

42 Baron-Cohen, S., Leslie, A., & Firth, U. (1985). Does the autistic child have a 'theory of mind'? *Cognition, 21*, 37–46. https://doi.org/10.1016/0010-0277(85)90022-8
43 Schroeder, S. R. (2018). Do bilinguals have an advantage in theory of mind? A meta-analysis. *Frontiers in Communication, 3*, 36. https://doi.org/10.3389/fcomm.2018.00036
44 Meltzoff, A. N., & Decety, J. (2003). What imitation tells us about social cognition: A rapprochement between developmental psychology and cognitive neuroscience. *Philosophical Transactions of the Royal Society of London. Series B: Biological Sciences, 358*(1431), 491–500. https://doi.org/10.1098/rstb.2002.1261
45 Slaughter, V. (2015). Theory of mind in infants and young children: A review. *Australian Psychologist, 50*(3), 169–172. https://doi.org/10.1111/ap.12080
46 Brown, J., & Whiten, A. (2000). Imitation, theory of mind and related activities in autism: An observational study of spontaneous behaviour in everyday contexts. *Autism, 4*(2), 185–204. https://doi.org/10.1177/1362361300004002006
47 Lin, S. K., Tsai, C. H., Li, H. J., Huang, C. Y., & Chen, K. L. (2017). Theory of mind predominantly associated with the quality, not quantity, of pretend play in children with autism spectrum disorder. *European Child & Adolescent Psychiatry, 26*(10), 1187–1196. https://doi.org/10.1007/s00787-017-0973-3
48 Charman, T., & Baron-Cohen, S. (1994). Another look at imitation in autism. *Development & Psychopathology, 6*, 403–413. https://doi.org/10.1017/S0954579400006015.
49 Edwards, L. A. (2014). A meta-analysis of imitation abilities in individuals with autism spectrum disorders. *Autism Research*, 7(3), 363–380. https://doi.org/10.1002/aur.1379
50 Gordon, R. G., Grimes, B. F., & Summer Institute of Linguistics. (2005). *Ethnologue: Languages of the world*. Dallas, TX: SIL International.
51 Blank, S. C., Scott, S. K., Murphy, K., Warburton, E., & Wise, R. J. (2002). Speech production: Wernicke, Broca and beyond. *Brain, 125*(8), 1829–1838. https://doi.org/10.1093/brain/awf191
52 Frank, M. C., Braginsky, M., Yurovsky, D., & Marchman, V. A. (2021). *Variability and consistency in early language learning: The wordbank project. Cambridge, MA: MIT Press. Retrieved from:* https://langcog.github.io/wordbank-book/index.html
53 Burns, T. C., Yoshida, K. A., Hill, K., & Werker, J. F. (2007). The development of phonetic representation in bilingual and monolingual infants. *Applied Psycholinguistics, 28*(3), 455–474. https://doi.org/10.1017/S0142716407070257

54 Kuhl, P. K., Stevens, E., Hayashi, A., Deguchi, T., Kiritani, S., & Iverson, P. (2006). Infants show a facilitation effect for native language phonetic perception between 6 and 12 months. *Developmental Science, 9*(2), 13–21. https://doi.org/10.1111/j.1467-7687.2006.00468.x
55 Adank, P., Hagoort, P., & Bekkering, H. (2010). Imitation improves language comprehension. *Psychological Science, 21*(12), 1903–1909. https://doi.org/10.1177/0956797610389192
56 Rizzolatti, G., & Arbib, M. A. (1998). Language within our grasp. *Trends in Neuroscience, 21*, 188–194. https://doi.org/10.1016/s0166-2236(98)01260-0
57 Aziz-Zadeh, L., Wilson, S. M., Rizzolatti, G., & Iacoboni, M. (2006). Congruent embodied representations for visually presented actions and linguistic phrases describing actions. *Current Biology, 16*, 1818–1823. https://doi.org/10.1016/j.cub.2006.07.060
58 Corballis, M. C. (2010). Mirror neurons and the evolution of language. *Brain and Language, 112*(1), 25–35. https://doi.org/10.1016/j.bandl.2009.02.002
59 Bandelow, B., & Michaelis, S. (2015). Epidemiology of anxiety disorders in the 21st century. *Dialogues in Clinical Neuroscience, 17*(3), 327–335. https://doi.org/10.31887/DCNS.2015.17.3/bbandelow
60 Beesdo, K., Knappe, S., & Pine, D. S. (2009). Anxiety and anxiety disorders in children and adolescents: Developmental issues and implications for DSM-V. *Psychiatric Clinics, 32*(3), 483–524. https://doi.org/10.1016/j.psc.2009.06.002
61 Kessler, R. C., Berglund, P., Demler, O., Jin, R., Merikangas, K. R., & Walters, E. E. (2005). Lifetime prevalence and age-of-onset distributions of DSM-IV disorders in the National Comorbidity Survey Replication. *Archives of General Psychiatry, 62*(6), 593–602. https://doi.org/10.1001/archpsyc.62.6.593
62 Beesdo, K., Pine, D. S., Lieb, R., & Wittchen, H. U. (2010). Incidence and risk patterns of anxiety and depressive disorders and categorization of generalized anxiety disorder. *Archives of General Psychiatry, 67*(1), 47–57. https://doi.org/10.1001/archgenpsychiatry.2009.177
63 Eley, T. C., McAdams, T. A., Rijsdijk, F. V., Lichtenstein, P., Narusyte, J., Reiss, D., Spotts, E. L., Ganiban, J. M., & Neiderhiser, J. M. (2015). The intergenerational transmission of anxiety: A children-of-twins study. *American Journal of Psychiatry, 172*(7), 630–637. https://doi.org/10.1176/appi.ajp.2015.14070818
64 Lester, K. J., Field, A. P., Oliver, S., & Cartwright-Hatton, S. (2009). Do anxious parents interpretive biases towards threat extend into their child's environment? *Behaviour Research and Therapy, 47*(2), 170–174. https://doi.org/10.1016/j.brat.2008.11.005

65 Sahu, M., & Prasuna, J. G. (2016). Twin studies: A unique epidemiological tool. *Indian Journal of Community Medicine: Official Publication of Indian Association of Preventive & Social Medicine, 41*(3), 177–182. https://doi.org/10.4103/0970-0218.183593

66 Waszczuk, M. A., Zavos, H. M., Gregory, A. M., & Eley, T. C. (2014). The phenotypic and genetic structure of depression and anxiety disorder symptoms in childhood, adolescence, and young adulthood. *JAMA Psychiatry, 71*(8), 905–916. https://doi.org/10.1001/jamapsychiatry.2014.655

67 Murray, L., Creswell, C., & Cooper, P. J. (2009). The development of anxiety disorders in childhood: An integrative review. *Psychological Medicine, 39*(9), 1413–1423. https://doi.org/10.1017/S0033291709005157

68 Creswell, C., Cooper, P., & Murray, L. (2010). Intergenerational transmission of anxious information processing biases. In J. A. Hadwin & A. P. Field (Eds.), *Information processing biases and anxiety: A developmental perspective* (pp. 279–295). Wiley. https://doi.org/10.1002/9780470661468

69 Cook, M., & Mineka, S. (1987). Second-order conditioning and overshadowing in the observational conditioning of fear in monkeys. *Behaviour Research and Therapy, 25*(5), 349–364. https://doi.org/10.1016/0005-7967(87)90013-1

70 Gerull, F. C., & Rapee, R. M. (2002). Mother knows best: Effects of maternal modelling on the acquisition of fear and avoidance behaviour in toddlers. *Behaviour Research and Therapy, 40*(3), 279–287. https://doi.org/10.1016/s0005-7967(01)00013-4.

71 De Rosnay, M., Cooper, P. J., Tsigaras, N., & Murray, L. (2006). Transmission of social anxiety from mother to infant: An experimental study using a social referencing paradigm. *Behaviour Research and Therapy, 44*(8), 1165–1175. https://doi.org/10.1016/j.brat.2005.09.003

72 Silvers, J. A., Callaghan, B. L., Van Tieghem, M., Choy, T., O'Sullivan, K., & Tottenham, N. (2020). An exploration of amygdala-prefrontal mechanisms in the intergenerational transmission of learned fear. *Developmental Science.* https://doi.org/10.1111/desc.13056

5

IMITATION IN ADOLESCENCE

INTRODUCTION

Imitation is at an all-time high during adolescence. Why? Remember that one function of imitation is to show that you want to belong to a group (see Chapter 2). You want to show that you follow the norms and values of the group. The best way to show that you care about a group is to copy the behavior of important group members. But why do you want to belong to a group so badly during adolescence? That is because adolescence is the most scaring time in your life! Why? Because you have got to find out who you are, that's why!

Once you become fully aware that you are *not* the same as your parents or once you become fully aware that you are a *unique individual*, you become scared. There are all these important existential questions creeping up: Who am I? What do I like? What do I dislike? Who are my friends? Who are my enemies? Where do I fit in? What is my role in society? With so much uncertainty at hand, it is logical that you try to find comfort in the group by imitating other group members.

In this chapter, we discuss how during adolescence friends become more important than family, how social media and celebrities play a crucial role during adolescence, and why adolescents can engage in all sorts of risky behavior, including violence. Then we draw conclusions about adolescence and imitation.

DOI: 10.4324/9781003175056-5

FRIENDS OVER FAMILY

When you were born, you were fully dependent on your parents (or other primary caregivers). You needed food, milk, warmth, and kisses. Thus, your parents clothed you, fed you, put you to bed when needed, walked around with you, played with you, etc. However, when you got older, you started to learn how to do things yourself. For example, you started eating from your own plate and you started to dress yourself. You have learned from those around you how to do this partly by imitation. Slowly but surely, you became less dependent on your parents for your primary care. And then at one point, you realize you do not want or need to do everything in the same manner as your parents have told you because you have got friends now!

This is a big step in your life! In adolescence, the influence of your parents on you declines, while the influence of peers on you becomes stronger.[1, 2, 3] This influence of your friends is strong in all sorts of domains. For example, peer influence can predict the development of depression. This can happen because when adolescents sit together, they may start ruminating together, which means that they share their problems and negative experiences. Thus, by imitating each other's rumination, they may collectively become depressed!

One interesting consequence of declining family influence and rising peer influence is the rise of all sorts of subcultures during adolescence.[4, 5] You can see this in hobbies. For example, adolescents may feel attracted to different kinds of sports. You can see subcultures for adolescents involved in cricket, hockey, ballet, soccer, etc. Similarly, there are different subcultures associated with different kinds of (social) media use: you can distinguish "gamers" and social media used for communicating with each other (e.g., WeChat in China or WhatsApp in various other parts of the world).

Interestingly, in terms of popular Western music, there have always been subcultures of young people imitating each other: from the rock and rollers in the 1950s; the hippies in the 1960s; the disco movement and the punks in the 1970s; the new wave scene, the hip-hop/rap movement, electronic dance music (including house, techno, rave, etc.) in the 1980s; and the grunge movement in the 1990s. In all cases, imitation plays a crucial role.

It is fascinating that oftentimes imitation in various subcultures involves physical elements, for example, clothing or hair style. People want to express their shared identity via physical means potentially because this stands out. This can be wearing dreadlocks for reggae artists or an "Afro hair cut" for people with an African background or wearing long hair for hippies. A clear example of the use of clothing/hair style can be seen in the first words of the popular song *San Francisco* by Scott McKenzie (written by John Phillips) in 1967. These words give a clear clothing instruction for anyone going to San Francisco to wear flowers in their hair. And adolescents in 1967 took that instruction seriously!

But being part of a youth culture oftentimes involves enthusiasm for new ideas as well. It can be very exciting to be part of a new subculture. That sounds so exciting – let's all go to San Francisco! And that's what many youngsters did, including the Beatles' group member George Harrison (which led to more imitation, as people tend to follow the steps of famous people).

Thus, when people move from childhood to adolescence, the influence of parents becomes weaker. All of a sudden, youngsters are more influenced by their peers. This influence might become apparent in the type of clothes that they start wearing. But this influence of peers on people's ideas, norms, and values can be just as strong.

CELEBRITIES AND SOCIAL MEDIA INFLUENCERS

In addition to friends and peers, what are the important sources of influence on adolescents? Two important sources of influence are celebrities and social media influencers.[6] First, people admire celebrities. They can be film stars, pop stars, royal stars, etc. There is a hint of circularity in the reasoning here: because we see them as stars, we want to know all about them and follow their clothing or ideas. But partly because we all want to follow them (e.g., via social media or traditional media outlets), they become stars. The old chicken-and-egg problem: which came first? Do we want to follow them because they are stars? Or are they stars because we all want to follow them?

Putting this question aside, it is clear that celebrities are in a good position to instigate imitation in their adolescent followers. Indeed, that is the reason why celebrities often are used in advertisements. But does it work? Yes, it does! For example, a study among 227 Indian students showed that celebrity ads were successful in making people wanting to buy the advertised product. This tendency was particularly strong when students found the celebrities attractive and credible, which strengthened their wish to imitate the celebrities. So, by the wish to imitate celebrities, people are lured into buying the products that the celebrities (willingly or by chance) advertise.

And, of course, this is the very reason why so many celebrities start their own commercial company during the height of their success or after a successful career (e.g., in sports). For example, in India, several successful ex-cricket players started their own commercial companies.[7] In the United Kingdom, ex-soccer players such as David Beckham started their own companies (in his case in clothing and perfume).

Second, across the globe, adolescents (and adults as we will see in Chapter 6) are increasingly influenced via social media by, uh, "influencers". These influencers will tell their followers about what they have been doing over the last couple of days or what they are doing at the moment or what they are up to in the near future. This can range from holidays, shopping, or meeting friends. Importantly, influencers, as the name suggests, have some ideas to convey. They might have a drink that they particularly like, or they might have a travel destination that they rave about or a new hair product that they find fantastic. Needless to say, they are getting paid by companies to tell these things in their video. These days they can do this via social media such as TikTok, Instagram, YouTube, or Twitter. But by the time you read this book, most likely there will be new trends and apps associated with influencers.

No matter which new app might appear, the central element of all these trends has been and will be: people start imitating celebrities because they admire them and want to be like them and think like them. Influencers influence people sometimes by telling them what kind of clothes to wear. At other times, they also influence people by telling them what kind of ideas to have.

Is this all very new and recent? No, not really. Fan clubs, for example, have always existed. In the 1960s, the Beatles fan club had

80,000 members in the United Kingdom alone. These members want to follow the steps of their heroes and, if possible, imitate them. What is new perhaps is the ease and speed by which trends can become global. Transfer of information has reached an all-time high. Within seconds, a news flash can be reported online and picked up all around the world (provided that it is not censored by your government). From that perspective, globalization has reached a high level. People in remote parts of the world can be influenced by the newest trends in the cities around the world.

Let's assume that you have a great product that you want to sell. Do you want to hire a celebrity or a social influencer to advertise your product? Well, you might want to go for the social influencer! Why? Because research shows that people actually identify more with influencers than with celebrities. They also feel more similar to influencers than to celebrities. And finally, people trust influencers more than celebrities.[8]

PEER INFLUENCE ON RISKY BEHAVIORS IN ADOLESCENCE

Mary is 13 years old, and her parents are amazed about the quick change: a year ago Mary was still enthusiastic about going camping on summer holidays with them in a tent. This year, her parents decided it was wiser to, instead of a tent, book a holiday house with sufficient access to Wi-Fi for Mary to be able to keep in touch with her friends through social media to see what they were doing during the holidays. Not only that, they invited two of Mary's friends over to also stay a couple of days. One day, Mary admitted that the night before she went to go for a swim in the middle of the night in the lake. It was something "all her friends did during the summer". "Our Mary", her parents say to each other, "do you remember that just a year ago she hardly dared to go around the house in the middle of the night by herself!".

Just as the psychoanalyst Sigmund Freud, the developmental psychologist Erik Erikson considered adolescence as a time of "storm and stress". The age between 12 and 18 years is the time where a person develops their identity. According to Erikson, adolescents have to come to terms with "who they are" and "who they are to be" in this world. According to Erikson, if adolescents do not succeed in this, they experience confusion which may result in lower psychological well-being.[9] As mentioned at the start of this chapter, adolescence is a time where the social environment changes. Adolescents spend more time with peers and less with their family. It is also the time where a shift occurs from the primary school to the secondary (high) school. New friends need to be made, existing friendships may be lost, and there is the risk of being excluded. As we have seen in the first part of this chapter, peers are of key importance to the development of identity. In trying to fit in, adolescents may subject to the norms of their peer group.

This can have positive consequences, of course. Adolescents explore new borders and try out new things inspired by fellow peers and imitating their ways. They may develop interests in studying, music, sports, or night swimming! Peers may also follow the example of role models, as Figure 5.1 shows. In the picture, we see the Swedish environmental activist Greta Thunberg who demonstrates against climate change. Her example motivated many adolescents worldwide to also engage in collective protest.

Figure 5.1 The Swedish activist Greta Thunberg engages in positive risk-taking behavior by protesting on the world stage against climate change; many other adolescents follow her example.

Source: shutterstock.com.

Peer influence can also have negative consequences. It can result in several forms of risky behavior. Indeed, risky behaviors are generally considered to be those behaviors that are not accepted in a society and are harmful to the person or the environment. This may differ from society to society, of course, but commonly mentioned examples of risky behaviors are related to drinking alcohol, smoking, sexual behavior, dangerous driving, and aggressive behaviors in school or the neighborhood. It can also result in more extreme behaviors such as delinquency, criminal behaviors, or engagement in extremist groups who use violence to reach their ideals as we will see later in this chapter.

Adolescence seems to really be a time of "storm and stress" as risky behaviors peak in adolescence, between 12 and 18 years old. Why adolescents are particularly prone to risk-taking behaviors has been investigated widely as we can see in Box 5.1. We now first focus on an important cause of risk-taking behaviors, namely peer influence.

BOX 5.1 WHY ARE ADOLESCENTS PRONE TO RISKY BEHAVIORS?

Risk-taking behaviors peak in adolescence. Why is this the case? Developmental psychologists have studied this question for a long time. In general, there are four different ways risky behavior in adolescence (in comparison with childhood and adulthood) can be understood.

The first one has to do with the development of *cognitive skills*. Cognitive skills involve memory and the ability to estimate risks. Compared to adults, adolescents seem to be less able to judge well the consequences of, for example, drinking too much or smoking. For example, compared to adults, adolescents *underestimate* the negative consequences of risky behaviors.[10] While cognitive skills play an important role in risk-taking behaviors, it does not seem to be the whole story.

A second explanation lies in *emotional development*. The emotions we feel when thinking about the risky behavior influences whether we engage in it or not. For example, if smoking will make me feel bad afterwards then I am not inclined to do it. But if it makes me feel better because I look cool in front of my friends, perhaps I will take it up nevertheless! According to this explanation, one reason why adolescents engage in risky behavior is that they tend to focus more on the positive feelings they expect in the short term. Adolescents are more impulsive than adults and are more likely to seek adventure and sensation. Impulsivity and sensation seeking are related to higher risk-taking in adolescence.[11] By focusing only on the expected positive feelings that follow a behavior, an adolescent may underestimate negative consequences. Adolescents are also less good in controlling their emotions compared to adults, which is also related to greater risk-taking.[12]

A third explanation is *biological development*. The functioning of our brain (think of how good we are able to control our emotions and how good we are of planning the future) is closely related to risky behaviors. For example, alcohol consumption is higher in adolescence than in adulthood. One reason for this is that those brain parts involved in estimation of risks and controlling emotions (an area called the *prefrontal cortex* plays a key role here) are not yet fully developed in adolescence.[13] However, it also works the other way around. Excessive alcohol usage worsens brain functioning. It can lead to impaired memory and reduces our ability to control emotions. The relation between risk-taking behavior in adolescence and brain functioning seems to work in both ways!

The fourth way the peak of risk-taking behavior can be understood is *social development*. This involves the social and cultural environment in which the adolescent grows up. This influence can be *direct* (i.e., peers providing alcohol or cigarettes) or *indirect* (i.e., observing others smoking or drinking). When their parents are actively involved and adolescents have a positive (secure) relationship with their parents, adolescents show *less* risk-taking behaviors. However, when adolescents are bullied by their peers or interact with peers who engage in risk-taking behaviors, they are *more* likely to show risky behaviors.[14]

Risk-taking behavior in adolescence is often related to behaviors which most people in societies see as something negative. It is, of course, also possible to view risk-taking behavior in a more positive light (*positive risk-taking behavior*). For example, adolescents prone to risk-taking behavior may excel in certain behaviors such as sports or music. Think of a young athlete performing at the Olympics, a young musician engaging in a contest in front of a large audience, or adolescents who take the global stage to protest such as the Swedish environmental activist Gretha Thunberg (see Figure 5.1).

The influence of peers is important in explaining other behaviors such as aggression, bullying, and carrying weapons. These behaviors have consequences for others, and we will discuss the role of peer influence in violent behavior in more detail later on. There are also risky behaviors that have direct negative consequences for adolescents. Not only smoking and alcohol use are examples, but also drug use, disordered eating behaviors, unhealthy body images, and depression.[15]

The first time a person smokes a cigarette, it makes them feel sick. So why do many adolescents pick up smoking? There are two general explanations for this. First, peer pressure plays a role. A peer may ridicule another person for "not joining in" with the group. For adolescents, it is particularly important to belong to a group, and whether peers approve or disapprove of a behavior strongly predicts behavior. In this way, peers directly influence each other, and we call this the *direct route* to risky behavior.

Another possibility, which we call *the indirect route to risky behavior*, is that an adolescent sees peers (or popular role models in music bands, movies, and social media) smoking and as a result also picks up the smoking behaviors to express that they also belong to the group and are similar to the others. Whereas both the direct and indirect routes lead to risky behavior, it seems that the indirect route is more important. For example, researchers interviewed 102 adolescents of 11–12 years old in Northern Ireland.[16] The adolescents lived in economically deprived areas. The researchers interviewed the same adolescents again several times during the following three years. They found that the adolescents they interviewed rarely picked up smoking through direct pressure. Instead, they picked up smoking mainly because they wanted to be like and behave similarly as their peers.

In the example above, the researchers used interviews to better understand the risky behavior. Another way to study risky behaviors is by doing experiments. For example, in one study, it was examined why adolescents engage in more risk-taking in traffic, alcohol use, and delinquency.[17] To examine this, the researchers used the so-called *stoplight game*. This is a computer game where participants view roads with a bird's-eye view, and they drive their car on the screen. When the participant approaches a section, the traffic light jumps from green (safe to continue) to yellow (you have to stop). Participants could brake by pressing the space bar or could continue with the risk of crashing with another car. Those participants who braked less were those persons who were higher risk-takers. Importantly, before the adolescents started the game, they were told that who finished the game the fastest in their school would get a prize. After the study, the adolescents completed a questionnaire measuring different risky behaviors.

The researchers found that those adolescents who were prone to taking more risks in the game (they pushed the brake less often) were also prone to take more risks in traffic in real life (crossing red lights with the bicycle). These adolescents also smoked more cigarettes and were more likely to use marihuana. They drank more alcohol and engaged more in delinquent behavior (damaging property, having been arrested by the police). Importantly, the researchers found that for boys, but not for girls, the presence of other peers when doing the game led them to take more risks. The study nicely shows how risk-taking can be studied, even in school settings. It also shows that peer influence on taking risks may work stronger for boys than for girls.

So, what can explain why the presence of peers influences taking risks? An important part of the story is the *social norm* and adolescents' *need to belong* to a social group. To feel included, it is important to behave like and look similar to others and avoid being rejected.[18] If peers start to drink alcohol, an adolescent becomes more motivated to copy this behavior in order to remain part of the group. Adolescents are also more likely to look at their peers when judging risks. Should I drink alcohol or not? In answering this question, adolescents look whether their peers drink alcohol and consider more what peers say about alcohol than what their parents do. *Feeling rewarded* also plays an important role. Think back of the stoplight game experiment described above. It is rewarding to see your peers looking at you in awe and with respect when you dare to take greater risks. This in turn motivates to keep on taking risks in the future.

SOCIAL MEDIA AND RISK-TAKING

Social media is an increasingly important area for adolescents to socialize with each other. The "online" and "offline" world of adolescents become increasingly connected. Experiences are shared through brief messages, videos, and photos. Adolescents intensively use social media to connect to peers and are occupied with how to manage the impression they make on others. This has consequences for risky behavior. As we have already learned, in adolescence risky behaviors peak and peers form a central role in their lives. Adolescents who use social media more are also more likely to engage in risky behaviors such as using drugs and alcohol and engaging in risky sexual behaviors.[19] For example, adolescents are more impulsive compared to adults and may put images of themselves online which they afterward regret. This can lead to feelings of anxiety and depression. Indeed, higher social media use among adolescents has been found to be linked to depression.[20] Luckily, however, the relation that researchers found is not very strong. This might mean that for most adolescents, social media is an enrichment to their lives.

But why is it that for some adolescents social media may lead to depression and risky behaviors and for others not? One answer lies in their personality. For adolescents who are confident and easily make friends, the online environment is an extra tool for doing so in addition to face-to-face interactions. Adolescents who are shy and do not find it easy to engage in face-to-face contact may also benefit from social media as they can get in contact with others. However, shy adolescents who feel anxious about meeting others also have less of a need to meet others offline. As a consequence, there is less face-to-face contact, which is important in finding their way in the world and dealing with the challenges that they face in adolescence.

Adolescents who use social media create an image of themselves that may not be realistic. In particular, girls tend to place those images of themselves online where they are most attractive. Girls share images of themselves and comment on images of other females discussing what should be considered the "ideal" body. The feedback they get from peers, in return, influences the way they look at themselves and how they judge others.[21] Concerns about how they look are related to experiencing low self-esteem and can result in feelings of depression, anxiety, and shame. This in turn can make it more difficult for a person to engage in meaningful friendships or romantic relations, which are particularly important in adolescence.

Social media is also a setting where social norms are formed. As in the real world, adolescents are *rewarded* when they follow the norm, so they imitate the behaviors of their peers. But if they do not follow the norm, there is the risk of being excluded. Adolescents tend, therefore, to follow those behaviors that they think will lead to acceptance of their peers. This need to feel accepted can make adolescents particularly vulnerable to images that are sensational or lead to unrealistic self-expectations. Indeed, it has been found that when adolescents see peers smoking or drinking alcohol online, they also tend to have a more positive attitude toward smoking and alcohol consumption.[22]

In sum, social media can be seen as an enrichment to the life of adolescents, but high social media use can result in risky behaviors and depression in some adolescents. Compared to children and adults, adolescents are more vulnerable to being influenced by others as they have a strong need to be included by their peers. In addition, they are prone to sensation seeking and risk-taking. One particular destructive form of risk-taking where imitation has been proposed to play a role is suicide, a behavior we turn to next.

COPYCAT SUICIDE

In 1774, the German writer and poet Goethe (1749–1832) wrote the book *Die Leiden des jungen Werthers* (*The Sorrows of Young Werther*) which tells about a young man who decides to take his own life after the girl he was madly in love with married another man. After publication, reportedly there was a suicide epidemic, with many young men and women following Werther's example. For fear of suicide imitation, the book was banned in the cities of Leipzig and Copenhagen, and there were discussions in society about whether the Werther suicide might be "contagious". Contrary to popular belief, fortunately, there was not a suicide epidemic, but there were a couple of imitation cases.[23] The "Werther effect" does live on nowadays under a different name, *copycat suicide*.

In Europe, suicide is the second leading cause of death among adolescents.[24] Adolescents seem to be particularly influenced by suicide thoughts that peers share and suicide attempts of their peers. If an adolescent has a peer who shares their thoughts about suicide or learns about a suicide attempt of a peer, then they start to think more about suicide themselves and are more likely to attempt suicide. For example, psychologists interviewed 118 adolescents and their parents.[25] Compared to adolescents who had no experience with peer suicide attempts or thoughts, adolescents who did have these experiences were more likely to attempt suicide themselves. Peers are not only a "risk factor" in regard to suicide thoughts and attempts but also an important source of prevention. Indeed, school-based programs have been developed to prevent suicide. In these programs, besides the training of staff, the peers are supporting each other after a suicide attempt. They can detect warning signs that a peer has thoughts about suicide. Also, they can set the norm for how to cope well with a difficult situation, for example, by stressing the importance to ask for help.

VIOLENT BEHAVIORS IN ADOLESCENCE

Besides engaging in risky behaviors directed at themselves, adolescents can be aggressive toward others. Aggressive behavior toward others already happens in childhood. For example, children get angry in the playground at primary school, and one child hits another child or pulls their hair. This is a direct, physical form of aggression. Interestingly, in adolescence, aggressive behaviors become less direct, less overt. Adolescents use more indirect, covert forms of aggression.[26] An example of these more indirect forms of aggression is spreading rumors about someone (gossiping). If you discover that people are talking negatively about you behind your back, you feel excluded and likely also angry, ashamed, or humiliated. Aggressive behaviors such as these are examples of ostracism. *Ostracism* is the phenomenon that a person is excluded from the social group.

That ostracism hurts has been shown by an ingenious study by psychologists.[27] Participants were put in an fMRI (functional magnetic resonance imaging) scanner. This is a machine that can locate the parts of the brain that are active when doing a particular task. When they were in this machine, participants could see a screen on which they saw two virtual people tossing a ball toward each other. At the start of this virtual ball-tossing game, the two virtual people threw the ball in the direction of the participant who could catch the ball with their virtual hands and throw it back. After a while though, the virtual peers did not throw the ball toward the participant. The participant was excluded from the game! Importantly, the results of the brain imaging showed that when this happened, similar brain areas became active that are also active even when people experience physical pain. In other words, being excluded literally hurts, even in this rather minimal situation of a virtual ball game! Social pain can be the same as physical pain, at least in the brain.

In adolescence, not only our social skills to hurt others but also our social skills to help others develop further. Compared to children, adolescents are better in mentalizing, emotion regulation, and resistance to peer influence.[28] Adolescents who are better at mentalizing can place themselves in the shoes of others. This is also called *perspective-taking*. Those adolescents who are better at this are better able to "read" other people. Those adolescents who are better at reading other people's minds are also less likely to be the victim of social exclusion because they can anticipate other people's intentions better.

Adolescents who are better at dealing with their emotions also tend to deal better with the negative feeling of being excluded. Instead of avoiding others and suppressing the negative feelings, they use different strategies. For example, instead of thinking "I am not worth anything, nobody likes me", they frame the situation as "that bully is just a pathetic person and does not know how to behave otherwise". These so-called *emotion regulation strategies* can also be trained. Seeing a negative event in a more positive manner can help adolescents deal better with negative situations and make them more resilient.[29]

Resistance to peer influence can also lead to helping behavior. Instead of imitating the behavior of bullies, a person may resist. For example, an adolescent who can better recognize whether another person is feeling sad or happy after being excluded is also more likely to help that person. Being a good emotion reader gives us tools to detect whether other people need help. In other words, those adolescents who are sensitive to signals of social exclusion are more likely to detect it if it is happening to peers around them. Instead of copying the behavior of the bullies, these adolescents may take a stand and therefore change the norm from bullying the victim to helping the victim. Better mentalizing and emotion regulation skills may therefore also counter bullying behavior.

COPYCAT SCHOOL SHOOTINGS

On April 20, 1999, two students entered their Columbine High School in Littleton, Colorado. They started shooting with semiautomatic rifles and pistols. They also had several explosives. Twelve students and a teacher were killed and 21 were wounded. The two youngsters (aged 17 and 18) who committed these acts committed suicide during their raid. Why did these adolescents engage in this so-called *school shooting*? Many reasons have been mentioned in the literature and popular media, including the possibility that the perpetrators themselves had a history of having been bullied. However, it is still unclear what their motives were; being socially excluded could have been one reason, but it is unlikely to have been the sole reason.[30] Bad parenting, a mental illness, and a traumatic experience in life – these factors can all play a role. School shootings are likely the result of many different reasons coming together. How the shooting is carried out, however, can be partly explained by imitation (Figure 5.2).

Figure 5.2 Students at Tucson High Magnet School (Tucson, Arizona – March 14, 2018) conduct a protest to commemorate the 17 victims of a school shooting in Parkland, Florida, as part of the national #ENOUGH! walkout day.

Source: shutterstock.com.

The Columbine school shooting seems to have inspired multiple other shootings.[31] For example, the perpetrator of a school shooting in the city of Santee, California, in 2001 had beforehand told his friends he was going to "pull a Columbine". Only several weeks later, he committed the attack.[32] Researchers examined this copycat behavior of school shooters in the United States between 1990 and 2017.[33] Comparing the different shootings that occurred in this period, they found that a school shooting was more likely to occur if it there had been other school shooting incidents in the neighborhood in the same year. This raises concerns that there are so-called *contagion effects*, the phenomenon that acts carried out by an individual are copied by others who observe that behavior. Indeed, school shootings receive abundant attention of (social) media whereby most of the attention is directed at the perpetrators, not at the victims.[34] This allows for contagion effects to occur. With the current rise in social media use, in combination with school shooters actually filming their acts and placing it online, it is likely that more copycat behaviors will occur. One way to reduce the number of school shootings would be to change the focus of the media, for example, by paying less attention to how the act was carried out. Also, once a school shooting occurs, other schools in the region should be warned to raise awareness that the act may be repeated in the near future.

COPYCAT TERRORISM

A last area of extreme imitation behavior is terrorism. Terrorists commit a terrorist act to receive (media) attention for their cause. Terrorist attacks are spectacular, shocking, and symbolic. As media attention is often providing detailed information about perpetrators and how acts were carried out, a copycat effect may therefore also be expected, just as is the case for school shootings. Indeed, terrorists may actually have the intention to inspire others to commit similar acts. There is some evidence that copycat behavior occurs in the realm of terrorism. For example, on July 14, 2016, a man drove into crowds celebrating Bastille Day in Nice, France, killing 86 people and injuring 458 others. Afterward, the perpetrator admitted that he had studied previous terror attacks in preparation.[35]

To answer the question whether international acts of terrorism are indeed contagious, the spread of international terrorism in between 1968 and 1974 was examined. The researchers counted 503 terrorist incidents in this period (bombings, kidnappings, assassinations, hijackings) which were conducted with a political motivation. They focused on the region of Latin America and Western Europe and found evidence that indeed terrorist attacks, in particular bombings and kidnappings, had contagion effects.[36] The contagion effect in terrorism has been widely discussed and investigated, but overall, it seems that terrorism is contagious, and the (social) media plays an important role in this.[37]

One particular interesting feature of terrorist groups is how they recruit new members. Terrorist groups often focus on young people, adolescents who are upset about injustice in the world. One afternoon in February 2015, three adolescent schoolgirls in Bethnal Green, London, never showed up for dinner at home. Instead, they boarded an airplane which took them to Istanbul in Turkey. From there, they traveled to Syria to join the Extremist Islamic terrorist group ISIS. It turned out that the girls followed the path another friend of them had taken earlier. A report from 2015 estimated that out of 4,000 Westerners who traveled to Syria and Iraq to join the extremist group ISIS, 550 were women and girls.[38] Importantly, the women and girls who joined were often adolescents, in their teens or early 20s. The extremist group particularly targeted young girls, focusing on their vulnerabilities and dreams and emphasizing that they as young Muslims were unjustly treated in Western societies and that they were being excluded. Through social media, other female members contacted the three girls, describing the lives they would have in Syria and that they should follow the example of other women.[39, 40] This example illustrates how extremist groups make use of the need to belong and feeling excluded from the society they lived in. Indeed, terrorist groups such as Al-Qaeda in that period looked for alienated and lonely youngsters and promised them companionship and solidarity of like-minded people if they would join the extremist group.[41]

In sum, terrorism seems to be contagious, in that terrorist acts may inspire others to copy them. But imitation plays another role as well as we have seen. Terrorist groups use strategies to recruit struggling adolescents who feel left out of society. Recruiters promise them a better life, giving examples of others who have gone before them and promising them a safe environment where they find like-minded others, companionship, and solidarity.

CONCLUSION

Adolescence is a time of storm and stress. As we have seen in this chapter, reasons for this is that adolescents feel uncertain about who they are and have a particular strong need to belong compared to children and adults. Following the example of peers becomes more important than listening to what the parents have to say. Social media plays a key role in this nowadays, with peers setting (unrealistic) examples and social influencers who adolescents tend to imitate. Importantly, risky behaviors peak in adolescence, which is partly due to a greater need for sensation. Suicide thoughts and attempts are being copied, but peers are also a source of preventing copycat suicides. Aggression is also observed, with adolescents showing more indirect aggressive behaviors such as gossiping. Feelings of social exclusion can lead to lower well-being in adolescents but are also a reason why extremist groups are successful in recruiting adolescents. All in all, imitation is a two-sided sword for adolescents: imitating peers gives them a handhold and a direction in life. But it can also be a source of risk. We ended this chapter with the developmental psychologist Erikson, who noted that the storm and stress associated with adolescence is an important challenge for all human beings to go through. If this challenge is met, and a strong identity is developed in this age period, then this provides a strong basis for the next developmental period: adulthood.

BOX 5.2 WHAT YOU SHOULD DEFINITELY REMEMBER FROM THIS CHAPTER

- When children get older, the influence of parents declines. They start imitating peers more often than their parents.
- Adolescents experience a lot of uncertainty because they have to find out who they are and form their own identities.
- This makes them particularly likely to imitate peers because that reduces their uncertainty.
- That gives rise to youth cultures all around the globe.

- Celebrities and social influencers are two other important sources of influence on adolescents. Adolescents often are inclined to imitate them.
- High social media use in adolescence is related to lower well-being due to risky behaviors and the setting of unrealistic standards about how to look or behave.
- Risky behaviors peak in adolescence; adolescents follow bad examples of others, but also good examples.
- School shootings and terrorist acts are contagious. Terrorist groups recruit adolescents by making them feel they belong to the group.

NOTES

1 Dishion, T. J., & Tipsord, J. M. (2011). Peer contagion in child and adolescent social and emotional development. *Annual Review of Psychology, 62*, 189–214. https://doi.org/10.1146/annurev.psych.093008.100412

2 Steinberg, L., & Monahan, K. C. (2007). Age differences in resistance to peer influence. *Developmental Psychology, 43*, 1531– 1543. https://doi.org/10.1037/0012-1649.43.6.1531

3 Wilkinson, R. B. (2004). The role of parental and peer attachment in the psychological health and self-esteem of adolescents. *Journal of Youth and Adolescence, 33*, 479–493. https://doi.org/10.1023/B:JOYO.0000048063.59425.20

4 McCracken, A. (2017). Tumblr youth subcultures and media engagement. *Cinema Journal, 57*(1), 151–161. https://doi.org/10.1353/cj.2017.0061

5 Schouten, A. P., Janssen, L., & Verspaget, M. (2020). Celebrity vs. influencer endorsements in advertising: The role of identification, credibility, and product-endorser fit. *International Journal of Advertising, 39*(2), 258–281. https://doi.org/10.1080/02650487.2019.1634898

6 Khamis, S., Ang, L., & Welling, R. (2017). Self-branding, 'micro-celebrity' and the rise of social media influencers. *Celebrity Studies, 8*(2), 191–208. https://doi.org/10.1080/19392397.2016.1218292

7 https://startuptalky.com/indian-cricketers-in-startup-ecosystem-2/

8 Schouten, A. P., Janssen, L., & Verspaget, M. (2020). Celebrity vs. Influencer endorsements in advertising: The role of identification, credibility, and Product-Endorser fit. *International Journal of Advertising, 39*(2), 258–281. https://doi.org/10.1080/02650487.2019.1634898

9 Erikson, E. H. (1968). *Identity, youth and crisis*. New York: W. W. Norton & Company, Inc.
10 Boyer, T. W. (2006). The development of risk-taking: A multi-perspective review. *Developmental Review, 26*(3), 291–345. https://doi.org/10.1016/j.dr.2006.05.002
11 Romer, D. (2010). Adolescent risk taking, impulsivity, and brain development: Implications for prevention. *Developmental Psychobiology, 52*(3), 263–276. https://doi.org/10.1002/dev.20442
12 Andrews, J. L., Ahmed, S. P., & Blakemore, S. J. (2021). Navigating the social environment in adolescence: The role of social brain development. In *Biological psychiatry* (Vol. 89, Issue 2, pp. 109–118). Elsevier Inc. https://doi.org/10.1016/j.biopsych.2020.09.012
13 Spear, L. P. (2018). Effects of adolescent alcohol consumption on the brain and behaviour. In *Nature reviews neuroscience* (Vol. 19, Issue 4, pp. 197–214). Nature Publishing Group. https://doi.org/10.1038/nrn.2018.10
14 Romer, D. (2010). Adolescent risk taking, impulsivity, and brain development: Implications for prevention. *Developmental Psychobiology, 52*(3), 263–276. https://doi.org/10.1002/dev.20442
15 Dishion, T. J., & Tipsord, J. M. (2011). Peer contagion in child and adolescent social and emotional development. *Annual Review of Psychology, 62*, 189–214. https://doi.org/10.1146/annurev.psych.093008.100412
16 Stewart-Knox, B. J., Sittlington, J., Rugkåsa, J., Harrisson, S., Treacy, M., & Abaunza, P. S. (2005). Smoking and peer groups: results from a longitudinal qualitative study of young people in Northern Ireland. *British Journal of Social Psychology, 44*(3), 397–414. https://doi.org/10.1348/014466604X18073
17 Defoe, I. N., Dubas, J. S., Dalmaijer, E. S., & Van Aken, M. A. G. (2020). Is the peer presence effect on heightened adolescent risky decision-making only present in males? *Journal of Youth and Adolescence, 49*(3), 693–705. https://doi.org/10.1007/s10964-019-01179-9
18 Andrews, J. L., Ahmed, S. P., & Blakemore, S. J. (2021). Navigating the social environment in adolescence: The role of social brain development. In *Biological psychiatry* (Vol. 89, Issue 2, pp. 109–118). Elsevier Inc. https://doi.org/10.1016/j.biopsych.2020.09.012
19 Vannucci, A., Simpson, E. G., Gagnon, S., & Ohannessian, C. M. C. (2020). Social media use and risky behaviors in adolescents: A meta-analysis. *Journal of Adolescence, 79*, 258–274. https://doi.org/10.1016/j.adolescence.2020.01.014
20 McCrae, N., Gettings, S., & Purssell, E. (2017). Social media and depressive symptoms in childhood and adolescence: A systematic review.

Adolescent Research Review, 2(4), 315–330. https://doi.org/10.1007/s40894-017-0053-4

21 Crone, E. A., & Konijn, E. A. (2018). Media use and brain development during adolescence. *Nature Communications, 9*(1). https://doi.org/10.1038/s41467-018-03126-x

22 Vannucci, A., Simpson, E. G., Gagnon, S., & Ohannessian, C. M. C. (2020). Social media use and risky behaviors in adolescents: A meta-analysis. *Journal of Adolescence, 79*, 258–274. https://doi.org/10.1016/j.adolescence.2020.01.014

23 Thorson, J., & Öberg, P. A. (2003). Was there a suicide epidemic after Goethe's Werther? *Archives of Suicide Research*, 7(1), 69–72. https://doi.org/10.1080/13811110301568

24 UNICEF (2021). *On My Mind: Promoting, protecting and caring for children's mental health. The state of the word's children 2021.* Regional brief. October 2021: United Nations Children's Fund. Retrieved from: https://www.unicef.org/eu/media/2021/file/State%20of%20the%20World's%20Children%202021.pdf

25 Singer, J. B., Erbacher, T. A., & Rosen, P. (2019). School-based suicide prevention: A framework for evidence-based practice. *School Mental Health, 11*(1), 54–71. https://doi.org/10.1007/s12310-018-9245-8

26 Dishion, T. J., & Tipsord, J. M. (2011). Peer contagion in child and adolescent social and emotional development. *Annual Review of Psychology, 62*, 189–214. https://doi.org/10.1146/annurev.psych.093008.100412

27 Eisenberger, N. I., Lieberman, M. D., & Williams, K. D. (2003). Does rejection hurt? An fMRI study of social exclusion. *Science, 302*(5643), 290–292. https://doi.org/10.1126/science.1089134

28 Andrews, J. L., Ahmed, S. P., & Blakemore, S. J. (2021). Navigating the social environment in adolescence: The role of social brain development. In *Biological psychiatry* (Vol. 89, Issue 2, pp. 109–118). Elsevier Inc. https://doi.org/10.1016/j.biopsych.2020.09.012

29 Wante, L., Van Beveren, M.-L., Theuwis, L., & Braet, C. (2018). The effects of emotion regulation strategies on positive and negative affect in early adolescents. *Cognition and Emotion, 32*, 988–1002. https://doi.org/10.1080/02699931.2017.1374242

30 Mears, D. P., Moon, M. M., & Thielo, A. J. (2017). Columbine revisited: Myths and realities about the bullying–school shootings connection. *Victims & Offenders, 12*(6), 939–955. https://doi.org/10.1080/15564886.2017.1307295

31 Lankford, A., & Tomek, S. (2018). Mass killings in the United States from 2006 to 2013: Social contagion or random clusters? *Suicide and Life-Threatening Behavior, 48*(4), 459–467. https://doi.org/10.1111/sltb.12366

32 T. McCarthy (2001). Warning: Andy Williams here. Unhappy kid. Tired of being picked. TIME, March 11, 2001. Retrieved from: http://content.time.com/time/magazine/article/0,9171,102077,00.html. Cited in: Franham, N. & Liem, M. (2017). *Can a copycat effect be observed in terrorist suicide attacks?* ICCT Research Paper, The Hague: March 2017.

33 Schweikert, K., Huth, M., & Gius, M. (2021). Detecting a copycat effect in school shootings using spatio-temporal panel count models. *Contemporary Economic Policy, 39*(4), 719–736. https://doi.org/10.1111/coep.12532

34 Dahmen, N. S. (2018). Visually reporting mass shootings: US newspaper photographic coverage of three mass school shootings. *American Behavioral Scientist, 62*(2), 163–180. https://doi.org/10.1177/0002764218756921

35 A. Nossiter et al. (2016). Years before truck rampage in Nice, attacker wasn't living in the real world. *The New York Times*, 24 July 2016. Retrieved from: https://www.nytimes.com/2016/07/25/world/europe/nice-france-bastille-day-attacks.html. Cited in: Franham, N. & Liem, M. (2017). *Can a copycat effect be observed in terrorist suicide attacks?* ICCT Research Paper, The Hague: March 2017.

36 Midlarsky, M. I., Crenshaw, M., & Yoshida, F. (1980). Why violence spreads: The contagion of international terrorism. In *Quarterly* (Vol. 24, Issue 2). https://www.jstor.org/stable/2600202

37 Nacos, B. L. (2009). Revisiting the contagion hypothesis: Terrorism, news coverage, and copycat attacks. *Perspectives on Terrorism, 3*(3), 3–13. Retrieved from: https://www.jstor.org/stable/26298412

38 Saltman, E. M. & Smith, M. (2015). *Till martyrdom do us part: Gender and the ISIS phenomenon*. London: Institute for Strategic Dialogue. Retrieved from: https://www.isdglobal.org/wp-content/uploads/2016/02/Till_Martyrdom_Do_Us_Part_Gender_and_the_ISIS_Phenomenon.pdf

39 De Freytas-Tamura, K. (2015). Teenage girl leaves for ISIS and others follow. *The New York Times*. February 24. Retrieved from: https://www.nytimes.com/2015/02/25/world/from-studious-teenager-to-isis-recruiter.html

40 Bennhold, K. (2015). Jihad and girl power: How ISIS lured 3 London girls. *The New York Times*. August 17. Retrieved from: https://www.nytimes.com/2015/08/18/world/europe/jihad-and-girl-power-how-isis-lured-3-london-teenagers.html

41 Sageman, M. (2004). *Understanding terror networks*. Philadelphia: University of Pennsylvania Press.

6

IMITATION IN ADULTHOOD

INTRODUCTION

Just as children and adolescents, adults maintain a strong need to belong to social groups. Indeed, decades of research in psychology have shown that it is a fundamental need. It has an effect on how we feel, how we think, and how we behave throughout our lives.[1] In adulthood, we like to meet with others regularly, we have long-term relationships with a spouse or several close friends, and we are member of a sports club and regularly meet with our fellow basket-ball or soccer friends. We play darts, sing in a choir, and go cycling in groups, and we work, recreate, and study together with our peers. Imitation plays an important role in building these social bonds. As discussed in Chapter 4, imitation helps children learn new skills, and build and maintain relationships from childhood into adulthood.

In this chapter, we will look at imitation in adulthood. The adult life span is the longest if we consider the different developmental stages throughout a human life. Adulthood covers the age range of about 18–60 years old (depending on the culture, some cultures consider adulthood starting at a sooner or later age). The topics and areas where we find imitation in adulthood are vast. We will first explore further the question why adults imitate others. We then pursue the idea that adults do not necessarily copy just anybody. It seems they are quite selective. Next, we explore examples of different areas where adults imitate each other. We discuss fashion (where imitation becomes visible), social media (in particular hypes), art, politics, and crowds. But as noted, there are

DOI: 10.4324/9781003175056-6

undoubtedly more areas in adulthood where imitation occurs. We will end this chapter with a discussion on cultural differences in imitation.

WHY DO ADULTS IMITATE?

Adults should know better than simply imitate others, shouldn't they? There may be a reason why adults keep on imitating others and *heuristics* provide part of the answer.[2] Heuristics are rules of thumb that help us navigate the complex social world we are living in. Throughout the day, adults are confronted with many choices: where to shop for groceries? Which mechanic to trust for repairing our bicycle or car? To which school should we bring our children? Should I work full-time or part-time? What shall I order in a restaurant? If you are in a restaurant and like to order pizza and are not sure what to choose, you may want to order the "pizza margherita" (mozzarella, tomato sauce, basil) as this is always a safe choice (and it is a good strategy to compare the quality of different Italian restaurants). Heuristics often do not help us find the best solution to problems or challenges we face. Instead, they help us find a *good-enough solution*. In many challenging situations, such as emergencies or a hectic period in the day, we do not have the time or resources to carefully consider all our options. In those situations, we look at other adults. Imitating the behavior of the majority of people in a social group saves time and energy. This may be particularly relevant in adulthood, as many adults have different responsibilities to manage at the same time such as a job, childcare, and chores around the house.

Indeed, humans are particularly well equipped to keep an eye on others and copy their behavior. We pay careful attention to what other people do and what other people look at. Indeed, as described in Box 6.1, it seems we even have specially developed mechanisms in our brain which are devoted to this skill. That is, humans are extremely sensitive to the face and in particular the eyes: what is my neighbor looking at? Not only humans have this tendency, we share this with other primates. But whereas monkeys seem to be focusing merely on the direction of the head, humans are more specialized: we are focusing on not only the head but also the gaze of other people.[3]

BOX 6.1 WHAT'S IN A FACE?

As discussed in Chapter 4 about imitation in childhood, we develop from an early age a preference to look at faces. It seems that our brain deals differently with faces than other objects such as flowers, cars, lamps, and fruit. Faces are processed "holistically", whereas these other objects are not. This means that faces (including the different features of eyes, nose, and mouth) are treated as "one". A flower, however, is treated as a combination of different features that together make the object. A consequence is that a face is not recognized by the brain as a face if the eyes are turned upside down. A flower, however, is still recognized as a flower even when its leaves are turned upside down. In sum, a face is recognized by the brain by perceiving it as a whole (holistically), whereas other objects are being recognized by the brain as a sum of their different parts.

Researchers have developed many measures to study the question whether faces, compared to other objects, are unique.

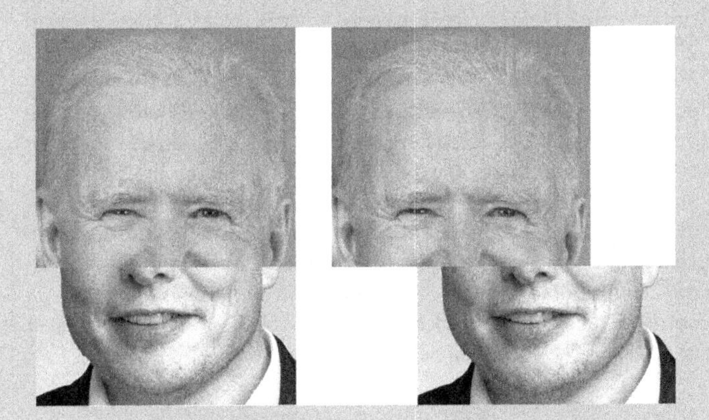

Figure 6.1 Two faces that are constructed to study the holistic processing hypothesis. The left face is the "composite arrangement", consisting of two halves of two faces: that of United States president Joe Biden and businessman Elon Musk that are combined into one new face. The right image shows a "non-composite arrangement", where the two face halves are misaligned. Example based on Young et al. (1987).

Source of the original picture of Joe Biden: https://www.whitehouse.gov/administration/president-biden/ and Elon Musk: Debbie Rowe, Photographer – accessed at wikimedia.org.

A landmark study was conducted in 1987.[4] In a series of ingenuous experiments, the researchers showed participants on a screen the top half of a famous face; nowadays, this could be the top half of United States president Joe Biden. They combined this top half with the bottom half of the face of another famous person, say businessman Elon Musk. They then created two images of these newly constituted faces: first, a *composite arrangement* where the two halves were aligned into one whole face, and second, a *noncomposite arrangement* where the two halves were misaligned. In that case, the bottom half of the face was placed a bit either to the left or to the right of the top half of the face. See Figure 6.1 for an example of stimuli used in the experiment (the faces shown in the original study were familiar faces in the United Kingdom at that time of the study).

The researchers found that the different halves were more easily recognized (they were named correctly more quickly) in the noncomposite arrangement than in the composite arrangement. In other words, when a face is presented as a whole (even though it consists out of two different halves), it is treated as a whole, instead of separate parts. This finding has been replicated in many studies.[5] Research over the past few decades has now confirmed that to recognize a face, we tend to treat faces as a whole, rather than depending on its different parts. It is interesting that we do *not* do this for other objects such as flowers or cars. This suggests that our brain is particularly effective in face recognition compared to other objects. Hence, our brains are programmed to pay special attention to human faces. This might be because these faces communicate important information. For example, it might tell us whether a situation is dangerous or not (which can be concluded from emotional expressions in a face) or where to find food (following the gaze of another person).

Watching what other people focus on is important for imitation. As noted, human beings are social and we "use" others to make decisions about how to behave. The tendency to imitate others comes at least partly from our tendency to use other people's behavior to make sense of complex or uncertain situations. This tendency is called *informational influence*. If other people run in a particular direction while the fire alarm is going off, you'd better also run into that direction. We follow others because they may know something that we do not. Indeed, one of the great advantages of following other people's behavior is that we don't need to know everything ourselves! We follow other people's examples based on the assumption that they know how to best handle the situation. This is related to one of the functions of imitation as described in Chapter 2: efficient learning. Another reason why people tend to follow others is called *normative influence*. As stated at the start of this chapter, social groups are crucial for our survival and well-being. But social groups themselves can only function well if group members follow the norms of the group at large. We therefore have a strong and possibly innate inclination to follow other people's behavior.

A classic study by the psychologist Solomon Asch demonstrated our tendency to conform (adapt) to others.[6] In his famous experiment, Asch brought together volunteer participants and paired each volunteer with six other volunteers. Each group got the simple task of judging the length of vertical lines, like the ones shown in Figure 6.2. A standard line was shown next to comparison lines.

Group members were then asked to identify the comparison line of the same length as the standard line. Each group member gave their answer out loud, one at a time in the order of seating.

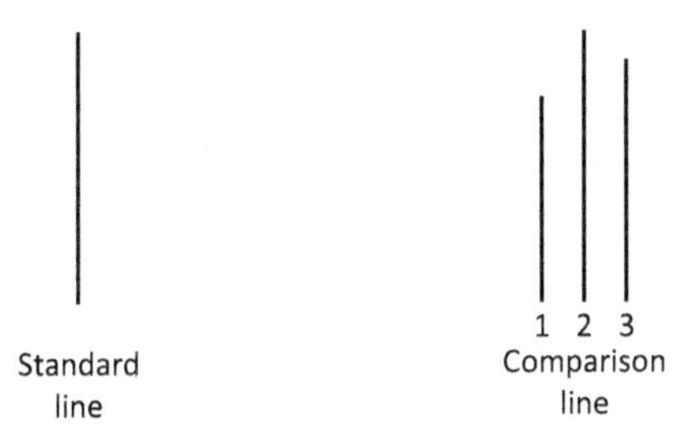

Figure 6.2 In the study by Solomon Asch (1956), groups of individuals were shown a standard line and comparison lines. Participants were then asked to select the comparison line that was of identical length as the standard line. This was repeated several times. On some occasions, the ones Asch was interested in, confederates in the study unanimously agreed on the wrong choice (in this case, line numbers 1 and 3). The majority of participants in the study conformed at least one time to the confederates, even if the choice was evidently wrong.

The experiment consisted of multiple *trials*: in each trial, a standard line was shown next to three comparison lines. What the volunteer student in each group did *not* know is that the other group members were *confederates*. That is, they worked together with Asch and had received instructions beforehand to all give a wrong answer. For example, in the trial shown in Figure 6.2, the confederates did not opt for line 2 (which would be the correct answer), but purposely all chose line 3 (which is incorrect). Asch was interested in the extent to which the volunteer participants would follow the confederates' choice in those so-called *critical trials*, where the answer was obviously wrong. Asch and his colleagues therefore made sure that the volunteer was seated second to last.

The results were striking: in one study, 75 out of the 100 participants followed the confederates in giving a wrong answer in at least one of the critical trials. Some individuals followed the confederates in all critical trials, showing a considerable amount of conformity, even though they were heavily doubting. The study has been repeated many times in multiple countries.

Studies like those conducted by Asch show the powerful effect of social norms in regard to imitation. One explanation of this phenomenon is that we tend to imitate others in a group in an effort to not stand out. We are very sensitive to the social norms of our group. We continuously ask ourselves whether a specific type of behavior is appropriate or not.[7] In other words, what are the social norms of the group and does my behavior fit in?

As discussed in Chapter 2, norms play an important role in regard to our behavior. The distinction between two kinds of norms is important when considering when people imitate other people's behaviors (see also Table 6.1).[8] First, there are *descriptive norms*. These norms tell us something about what is usually done by other people who belong to our group. Keep in mind that this group can be small, such as other people in the supermarket isle around you. But it can also be very large such as all the people in a country. If we see that other people wait for their turn before the checkout, we tend to do so too. But if the majority of customers do not, we may be tempted to follow their example.

Table 6.1 An overview of two types of social norms, associated behaviors, and situations in which these norms typically occur

Social norm	*Behavior*	*Situation*	*Example*
Descriptive norms	Take behavior of other people as a guideline for one's own behavior. Imitation of amoral behavior is higher likely.	Typical in situations where people do not have time or energy to consider their actions	A person cycling back from work being tired notices much litter in the park and throws away a candy wrapping on the ground without feeling guilty about it.
Injunctive norms	Avoid punishment or social disapproval. Imitation of amoral behavior is less likely.	Typical in situations where people have the time and energy to consider what they find important or not	A person throws away the candy wrapping and notices that many other people frown their eyebrows at this behavior.

The second type is called *injunctive norms*. These norms tell us what most people approve or disapprove of or what *ought* to be done. For example, during the COVID-19 pandemic, authorities told citizens to isolate when having flu symptoms. People going out to the supermarket when sneezing and coughing would have resulted in a lot of angry looks or people going out of your way is an example of the injunctive norm: you should not go out in public when sneezing and coughing. When COVID-19 infections went down, things eased in many countries, and people could sneeze freely again in the supermarket. The injunctive norm to stay home was gone.

Now, when do people pay attention to, and are they more likely to follow the norms? Motivation seems to play an important role here.[9] If we feel tired, we do not have enough energy or motivation to carefully think about the consequences of our behavior or about what other people think about our actions. When we simply follow others, we tend to follow the descriptive norms. But when we *do* have the time and are willing to spend some effort, we are more likely to follow the injunctive norm.

WHO DO ADULTS IMITATE?

We now learned that other people are strong influencers of our behavior. But, as *influencers* on social media show, some people seem to attract more attention than others. Influencers not only target adolescents, as discussed in Chapter 5, but also target adults. For example, in 2022 the top influencer was Cristiano Ronaldo, a Portuguese soccer player who had more than 440 million (!) followers on Instagram. At the time of writing this chapter, a commercial post on his account would cost more than 2.3 million dollars according to social media analytics companies.[10] It should hereby be noted that a soccer player may not be a real influencer. Nowadays, influencers are people who share pictures or videos related to products, and this is their full-time job (the so-called *content creators*). Nevertheless, we take this example because we assume that if millions of people follow a person, then this person by definition is an influencer (who also carries out a different profession, in our example being a soccer player).

So, what makes Cristiano Ronaldo so attractive? To answer this question, we have to go back to Chapter 2 where we discussed social learning, that is, learning by observing others. By looking at other people, we can save ourselves time and energy to learn new things. It pays off, often, to look at others who we deem to be experts in something. Cristiano Ronaldo may have become an influencer first of all because of his talents in playing soccer, being able to do something extraordinary what many other people are not able to do. Learning a technical soccer move by watching videos of Ronaldo playing soccer may pay off for our soccer skills. However, many followers of Ronaldo may not be that interested in soccer. Indeed, pictures of him posting with his family attracted at least as many followers as pictures related to soccer. An ultrasound image of the unborn twins of Ronaldo in 2021 earned him over 21 million "likes" at the day of publication.

But there is more to that. People like to compare themselves to others to learn more about themselves. Indeed, a classic psychological theory by Leon Festinger about social comparison helps us understand better why this is the case. Festinger's theory of social comparison states that we often compare ourselves to others, but some people are more relevant.[11] Then, who do we compare ourselves to? According to Festinger, there are two types of comparison: upward social comparison and downward social comparison. *Upward social comparison* involves those people who are better than you in some domain. They can be a source of inspiration, or a source of discouragement. Take Ronaldo, for example, if I would compare my soccer skills to his, I would be heavily discouraged. So, it may be better for me to compare myself, and imitate, the behaviors of other mortals who are closer to me in the domain of soccer skills.

The second type is *downward social comparison*. This involves comparing ourselves to people who are less skilled on certain tasks or may be less fortunate in another sense. We may be less likely to imitate their behaviors (as they are less skilled). However, it can make us feel good sometimes to compare ourselves to others who are less well-off. For example, people suffering from a mild form of breast cancer compare themselves with people suffering from more extreme forms of cancer ("At least I don't have cancer in my lungs").[12]

In regard to imitation, Festinger's theory would predict that we are more likely to imitate individuals who are better than us on some tasks (the upward comparisons) than those who are less well (the downward comparisons). But it also explains why we do like to compare ourselves with the less fortunate – when we feel bad about ourselves. We will now explore several areas where adults imitate each other. We will start with the area of fashion.

EXAMPLE 1: FASHION – IMITATION BECOMES VISIBLE!

Think of how adults dress themselves today and now compare this to 100 years ago. You will notice considerable differences. For example, at the start of the 20th century, in Western countries both men and women wore hats in public. Nowadays, this is a rarity. In Eastern countries such as Japan, the *kimono* was a common dress in public. Nowadays Japanese mostly dress in Western style, and the *kimono* is worn only on special occasions such as weddings. Whereas hats and *kimonos* were the fashion dress, people could still distinguish themselves. For example, the color, shape, and patterns of a *kimono* can vary greatly. Fashion, therefore, shows an interesting contrast in regard to imitation. On the one hand, people like to follow the norm of how to dress. On the other hand, people like to distinguish themselves from others. Fashion is in that way an important manner to express both our personal (who you are as a person) and social identities (which group you belong to).

Fashion can be seen as a messenger. It signals to our environment messages such as what we believe (think about a Muslim woman wearing a veil), and it tells something about our gender (women who wear dresses, men who wear a suit and tie), our ethnicity (indigenous women in the Andes who dress in layers of bright and colorful clothing), and our status. Typically, across cultures, people of high social status wear clothing which is designed by famous designers and often made of rare fabrics which take skill and time to produce. Even nowadays where clothing production is typically a process of mass production, this is evident. Think of a tailor-made suit or dress.

Through history, individuals who were well-off often had multiple types of garments, while those of lower social status only had one garment available. Take the Anglo-Saxons (a cultural group in England in the early Middle Ages) as an example. Archaeological excavations of graves show that high-status individuals owned gold buckles and brooches. They had multiple garments (i.e., being buried with two pairs of shoes) and high-quality clothing which involved time and skill to make. In all these examples, imitation plays a key role. Individuals imitate others' dress who are like themselves. Interestingly, there is evidence that cultures imitate other cultures in the past about how to show status. To stick with our Anglo-Saxon example, the dress of high-status individuals resembled the earlier Roman tradition including pairs of shoulder-clasps to fasten protective garment of roman style.[13] At the time of writing, in Western countries, dress styles from the 1990s and early 2000s are starting to be popular again, which were originally based on the 1970s.

In essence, therefore, fashion can be seen as a paradox.[14] On the one hand, fashion seems to go against all reason. Think about wearing high heels on a cobbled street or some people's brave efforts to maneuver their all-terrain four-wheel-drive vehicle through the city center trying to find a parking space. While fashion sometimes goes against all common sense, it shows us that people actually behave as the custom wants us to do. And what that custom is depends on whether you are rich or poor, young or old, the boss or an employee. In that sense, fashion shows the unwritten expectations about how to behave in society. Wearing uncomfortable clothing makes no sense at first sight, but if you consider the motivations behind it, it suddenly becomes sensible. Imitating others in terms of dress or behaviors helps to tell others in society who you are and where you belong. Of course, it can also be that a person imitates social classes they do not belong to but is motivated to belong to. For example, a low social status person who dresses up to make it seem they belong to a higher social class. So, answering the question why somebody imitates others (whether it is others from the present or the past) uncovers much about the unwritten societal rules and a person's (desired) place in society.

EXAMPLE 2: HYPES AND SOCIAL MEDIA IMITATION

A specific type of fashion is a *hype*. A hype is defined in the dictionary as "a feeling of expectation and desire for a particular thing to happen". In 2014, an initiative occurred on social media which showed that hypes can take large proportions very quickly around the world (it can go *viral*). It was called the *Ice Bucket Challenge*, an initiative which aimed to gather funding to combat the disease amyotrophic lateral sclerosis (ALS). This is a disease that affects neurons in the brain and the spinal cord which leads to reduced control of muscles. People may eventually lose their ability to speak, eat, move, and breathe. In the United States, it affects 30,000 individuals, with 5,000 new cases diagnosed each year. The Ice Bucket Challenge started in the US where golfer Charles Kennedy poured a bucket of ice water over himself to ask for attention for ALS and challenged people worldwide to do the same.

The Ice Bucket Challenge led to millions of followers on social media worldwide including famous people such as television personality Oprah Winfrey in the United States; the soccer player

David Beckham and his wife, singer Victoria Beckham, in Britain; the Hong Kong singer, actor, and film producer Andy Lau; the South African celebrity Bonang Matheba; and the soccer player Neymar in Brazil. The challenge led to an extraordinary increase of funding for the ALS foundation (more than 115 million dollars in 2014). It is a powerful demonstration of how imitation behavior through social media can be used to reach certain objectives.

So why was this hype so effective? According to the *STEPPS (Social currency, Triggers, Emotions, Practical value, Public, and Stories) model*, there are six elements why information is *catching* and can lead to imitation behavior.[15] The first is *social currency*. People are motivated to look good in front of others. In the case of the Ice Bucket Challenge, it is self-evident as people demonstrated to conduct an extraordinary act for a good cause.

Second, a *triggering event* is required to start the spread of information. In our example, it was a professional golfer who triggered the movement by making a brief video and putting it on social media.

Third, *emotions* play an important role. The challenge involved positive emotions (admiration, awe, humor, excitement) which helped capturing attention leading to a greater likelihood that the event would spread over social networks.

The fourth element refers to *public*. Information that has gone viral (or "public") is likely to tell us about the social norm about how we should behave and to imitation of that behavior. It hereby helps to have a concrete, well-described action that is easily repeated, such as pouring a bucket of ice water over yourself.

Fifth is *practical value* which is related to the tendency of humans to pass along practical or useful information to others in order to help them. Other people are using this information because they are given by particular sorts of people such as celebrities. As we discussed earlier, people tend to imitate celebrities because we admire them and like to be like them. It shows, again, that people in their decisions are not as rational as they like to think themselves to be. We tend to use heuristics (taking celebrities as a reference point) which lead to imitation.

Finally, there is the aspect of *stories*. People use stories to teach others and learn from them. Stories serve as vessels of information, and these vessels travel best when they contain simple but catching stories. The Ice Bucket Challenge is an example of that.

There is another type of imitation behavior that is less positive. We tend to imitate celebrities. However, this *prestige bias* (which was discussed in Chapter 2) has a dark side. Suicide is the second important cause of death (after accidental death) among young men across the world. It is more common among young men who suffer from psychiatric illness (i.e., depression, schizophrenia), who use substances (drugs), who are less well of economically, who live in the rural areas (compared to urban areas), and who are single. An important cause predicting suicide is the media reporting of other suicides, in particular those of celebrities. Research has shown that when celebrities commit suicide, this is often followed by a wave of copycat suicide attempts by their fans. For example, a study focusing on 98 different suicides by celebrities showed an increase in suicide rates among young men (aged 19–30 years) shortly after the celebrity suicided was reported in the media.[16] Their study looked at different cases in Asia, North America, Australia, and Europe. Noteworthy, deaths of celebrities abroad had lower copycat effects than when the celebrities were of the same nationality as the youngsters.

Differences across continents were also found, with higher copycat effects in North America and Europe than in Asia or Australia. This means that when 2,600 North American men would commit suicide on average per month, this number would be 4,264 after a celebrity death. It is important, therefore, to be aware of this dark side of imitation. Countermeasures against this celebrity suicide imitation can be taken. For example, this can be done by introducing guidelines for reporting on suicide in the media, which could include information on help-seeking options.

EXAMPLE 3: IMITATION AND ART

In the summer of 1975, a movie came out that shook audiences worldwide. *Jaws* (Steven Spielberg, 1975) showed a killer shark terrorizing the summer bathing resort Amity Island in the United States. It became the first "summer blockbuster" and one of the early successes of Hollywood. One of the film's producers, David Brown, said: "Almost everyone remembers when they first saw Jaws. They say, I remember the theatre I was in, I remember what I did when I went home – I wouldn't even draw the bathwater."[17]

The movie attracted millions of people into the cinema worldwide. Besides that, it led to many people being hesitant to swim in the water out of fear of sharks, the fact that so many people visited the cinema is an example of imitation behavior in itself. The movie became a hype with many of the characteristics discussed earlier. The movie spurred curiosity and instilled exhilaration and fear (*emotions*). It is a movie you "had to see", and it is the social norm (*public*). And it was the movie everybody talked about (*stories*). Importantly, the movie also may have instilled fear in many persons, tapping into the *practical value* element – the water may be dangerous, and it contains sharks. Better stay out! Noteworthy, the actual practical value can be argued about. The likelihood of being killed by a shark is much lower than that of being killed in a car accident.

Another part of imitation coming from art is that it influences our preferences. Movies are an example of a setting where *product placement* occurs. Think about Agent 007 in the James Bond movies who wears a particular watch brand and drinks a certain beer brand (instead of his normally preferred martini). These are examples of how companies "place" their product in a movie with the aim to increase the sales. It is built on the idea that a person we admire is the hero (think again of upward social comparison) and this admiration will lead to imitation behavior in its audience. In the movie industry, this started already in the 1890s where the French filmmakers Auguste and Louis Lumiére teamed up with a soap manufacturer. Not long after that "Sunlight Soap" prominently appeared in front of a tub in a movie scene with two women doing a handwash of laundry.[18] Product placement nowadays is also used by influencers which we discussed earlier in this chapter. They often include information links such as "#ad#sponsored".

Product placement builds on the underlying mechanism of imitation. First, it involves social learning and comparison processes. For example, the year after James Bond drove the BMW Z3 roadster car in the movie *Golden Eye*, the car became a big success. Worldwide the sales exploded and celebrities including the singer Madonna purchased the car (which in all likelihood spurred sales further among female fans). The psychological mechanisms of *social learning*, *social comparison*, and *social norms* evidently also play an important role here. The audience sees their hero (James Bond) using the car throughout the movie, the subsequent sales increase led to the perceived norm that this is the car that many other (successful) people drive, making it the descriptive norm.

Also, why do we visit certain museum and why do so many people like to have a picture of Van Gogh's *Sunflowers* on the wall? Besides that, a visit to a museum or watching a specific painting is a source of positive emotions and can make us feel good, we also visit these museums because other people do so and talk about it. Again, if certain role models in society do so, it can trigger our behaviors. A good example is former president Barack Obama's visit to the Rijksmuseum in Amsterdam in March 2014. The photo of Obama in front of Rembrandt's painting *De Nachtwacht* (*The Night Watch*) made headlines worldwide and spurred the number of visitors of the museum in the following year.

EXAMPLE 4: WHO DO YOU VOTE FOR? IMITATION IN POLITICS

Think back of the last political election you were eligible to vote in. Did you go out to vote or not? And to what extent do you think whether your decision to go out and vote (or not) was influenced by your partner or another family member in your household who was eligible to vote? Based on the existing research, it is likely that your decision was influenced by others in your social network. We imitate our friends, family members, neighbors, and coworkers. One experiment showed this in an elegant manner.[19] The researchers rang the doorbell of registered voters in the cities of Denver and Minneapolis in the United States during the 2002 Congressional Primaries. Half of the residents who answered the door received a message from the interviewer to go out and vote. The other half got a short information message about recycling (this was a control group). What was of interest to the researcher was how many of the residents that did not answer the door (the other members of the household) turned out to vote. The results showed that a person who originally had a 25% likelihood to vote would become 85% likely to vote, if the other residents in the house, who had received the "go out to vote" message, indeed went out to vote. It seems that other people in the household are quite influential in influencing our voting behavior.

In another study in Denmark, the voting behavior of 145,000 young adults was investigated.[20] The researchers were interested in the question whether young people who "leave the nest" copy the voting behavior and preferences of their parents. The study showed that the influence of their parents' voting habits decreased, while the influence of their peers of the same age increased. That is, in the four years after young adults in the study left the parental home, the likelihood that they would go out and vote dropped with 18%. Evidently, before young voters leave their parental house, they are positively influenced by their parents to vote. However, after leaving the home, peers become the more important source of imitation. Interestingly, after age 21, when the young adults settle down and start families of their own, voting behavior increased again. Again, social networks seemed to play a key source of information about whether to vote or not, or whom to vote for.

EXAMPLE 5: IMITATION IN CROWDS AND HELPING BEHAVIOR

Suppose you are shopping, you are in a dressing room in a store trying out a pair of trousers. Suddenly the fire alarm goes off. With your new trousers on, you run out of the locker room to see what is going on. People are running toward the emergency exit, and you decide to follow them. While you are speeding your way toward the exit, you pass other shoppers who seem to be frozen in the situation, panicking, not knowing what to do. Would you stop to help these people find their way out of the building, possibly endangering your own life? Or would you ignore them? Would it differ if these people who are standing around would be people you know, like members of the same sports organization as you? Or would that not make a difference? And where does imitation come into play in crowd behavior?

Questions like these crowd researchers are trying to answer. Crowds can be seen as the "elephant man" of the social sciences. Crowds are often considered to be something strange, something pathological, something monstrous. But crowds at the same time are viewed with awe and fascination.[21] Imagine you are taking part in a peaceful protest. Suddenly, protesters around you start to throw stones at the police. Would you imitate them and join in or not?

The attack on the Capitol (sometimes described at the heart of democracy) in Washington in the United States on January 6, 2021, is an example of how crowds can become quite extreme in their behavior. Traditional views of crowds assert that people are likely to lose part of their individuality which leads to behaviors they would otherwise not show. According to these theorists, even calm persons might start throwing stones when they see their fellow protesters doing so. Research on crowd behavior goes back to Gustave Le Bon's *La psychologie des foules* [*The Psychology of Crowds*] which came out in 1895. Le Bon observed that

> The most striking peculiarity presented by a psychological crowd is the following: Whoever be the individuals that compose it, however like or unlike be their mode of life, their occupations, their character, or their intelligence, the fact that they have been transformed into a crowd puts them in possession of a sort of collective mind which makes them feel, think, and act in a manner quite different from that in which each individual of them would feel, think, and act were he in a state of isolation.
>
> (pp. 24–25)

In other words, according to Le Bon, individuals lose part of their personal identity (those elements that make up who you are as a person and what you find important) when they find themselves in a crowd. According to Le Bon, individuals feel less responsible for their behavior. They also show less fear of punishment when they do something wrong.

The famous psychiatrist Sigmund Freud (1856–1939) was also interested in crowds. In his 1921 book *Massenpsychologie und Ich-Analyse* [*Psychology of Crowds and Self-Analysis*], Freud remarks that while Le Bon suggested that individuals in a crowd belong to a "collective mind", a unity, there must be something that connects these individuals (p. 9). Freud tried to find an answer by focusing on the individual by asking the question how the crowd changes an individual. According to Freud, in a crowd people are more ruled by emotions and less by rationality. People act less as an individual, their thoughts and feelings are focused in one particular direction, and there is a felt need to act on the subconscious impulses (p. 68). These impulses may be a subconscious need for aggression or love for a strong leader.

The well-known psychologist Philip Zimbardo posed in 1970 that crowds make individuals feel anonymous. And this anonymity makes it more likely that individuals in crowds will show antisocial behavior. Other researchers suggest we should have a more "dynamic" view of crowd behavior. For example, the Social Identity Model of Crowds suggests that individuals are influenced by others in the crowd but also by other social groups such as the police who tries to contain crowds and prevent disorder. When police use violence and repression against crowd members, also nonviolent crowd members can feel targeted and may come to see the police as the opposition. They thereby may move to imitate more extreme behaviors they would otherwise not do. To prevent this negative spiral, police officers should imitate the demonstrators by joining the crowd and engaging in dialogue, while arresting extreme individuals to prevent further spread of violence.

In sum, the question why individuals imitate other people in crowds has been the topic of discussion for more than a century. Whereas earlier accounts viewed crowds as mindless and dangerous entities, nowadays psychologists view crowds as dynamic entities. The individual's behavior depends on other people's behavior within the crowd, but also the larger social context.

EXAMPLE 6: IMITATION IN EMERGENCY SITUATIONS

Early March 2020, when the COVID-19 virus was first soaring around the world, an interesting behavioral phenomenon occurred that troubled the lives of many an adult: shortage of toilet paper in supermarkets. There was a run on toilet paper so the shelves in the supermarkets quickly emptied. Indeed, in the Netherlands, the Prime Minister, Mark Rutte, saw it necessary to tell citizens to relax and that "there is enough toilet paper for 10 years".[22] In Australia, the minister of agriculture wrote "Don't panic, Australia. The coronavirus doesn't mean we'll run out of food" and asked citizens to "stop stockpiling".[23] And in Singapore too the Prime Minister Lee Hsien Loong saw it necessary to release a message assuring his citizens that there were "more than enough supplies" to stop Singaporeans rushing to supermarkets to stock groceries (Figure 6.3).[24]

Figure 6.3 Empty shelves in a supermarket during the COVID-19 virus crisis.
Source: shutterstock.com.

Studies on how people behave in emergency situations can tell us a lot about why individuals act "irrationally". It turns out that whereas this behavior seems irrational at first glance, this behavior is actually quite functional and, in that sense, rational.[25] When we find ourselves in a situation that we perceive as threatening or uncertain, we are likely to look at others and what others pay attention to (see also Chapter 1).

To study how people behave in crowds, psychologists created a computer game to simulate emergency situations.[26] In this simulation, participants took on a character in the game which moved through an underground railway station. Participants received the information that a fire broke out and there was an urgent evacuation. This urgency was demonstrated by a "danger bar" indicating the time they had left to come out alive. While fleeing the situation, participants received help requests from others. Helping them would mean a delay to one's own safety.

The researchers created two versions of this game. In one version, participants were asked to think of themselves as unique, independent persons. Other characters in the simulation were described as "a crowd of shoppers". In the other version, participants were asked to think of themselves as a fan of a specific soccer team. In this version, the other characters were described as fans of the same soccer team. The results showed that there was more helping behavior when participants saw other characters as members of the same group.

One explanation of this finding is that when people see themselves as members of the same group, they start to share a same social identity. In other words, they "become one". This phenomenon, called *identity fusion,* has important implications for our behavior in social groups.[27] When we feel "oneness" with other group members, we are more likely to engage in behaviors that help others. We do so even stronger when others are close others such as family members. We are not only more likely to show pro-social behaviors but also more likely to trust others and their judgments. This increases the likelihood that we imitate other people's behaviors, even when it is irrational or not in line with our own morals and values.

IMITATION AND CULTURE

We have now reviewed several day-to-day examples of imitation in adult settings. An important question which we have not yet addressed is whether imitation *differs* across cultures. Do we find imitation in all cultures around the world? Is imitation of another person's dress appreciated equally among people who were born and raised in the US compared to people who were born and raised in Japan? And are people who violate a social norm (so do *not* imitate other people's behavior) judged differently in China versus the United States? A brief answer to these large questions is that overall, across nations and cultures, people tend to bond with others and learn from them, and imitation plays an important role in this. Imitation plays an important role in the development of *culture*, and it helps us sharing our customs and beliefs with other people.[28] In other words, imitation allows for social learning and occurs in all cultures around the world. However, whether imitation is valued or not can differ across cultures as we will see below.

Cultures can differ in the appreciation of imitation behavior. But why is this the case? A useful distinction that can be made is between so-called *individualistic cultures* and *collectivistic cultures*. The United States is an example of an individualistic culture. Countries such as China and Japan are examples of collectivistic cultures. Individualistic cultures are those cultures where individuals value personal happiness (so your own well-being) more than social happiness (happiness of other people). Also, individuals in individualistic cultures tend to be more *egocentric*. They tend to think more about themselves without regard for other people's feelings and desires. In collectivistic cultures, the happiness of the social groups that people belong to is more important. In these cultures, people are more *other-centric*: they think more about other people's feelings and desires. People in individualistic cultures tend to value more their uniqueness and independence.[29] East Asian people, in contrast, are happier when their relations and similarities to others are clear. In everyday life, this can be seen, for example, in dress. In the United States, people are more likely to value and enjoy diversity and emphasize uniqueness in fashion. Copying another person's dress is less likely to be appreciated by others than it would be in Japan or China.

Another important distinction that can be made across cultures is the *tightness or looseness of cultures*. "Tight" cultures typically have strong norms about how to behave (or not to behave), and there is a low tolerance for behavior that goes against the norm. "Loose" cultures have weaker norms about behavior, and people in these cultures tend to be more tolerant of deviant behavior. A comparison of 33 nations around the world shows that cultures that are typically "tight" are India, Pakistan, South Korea, and Singapore. Examples of "loose" cultures are the Netherlands, Belgium, and the United States. In regard to day-to-day behavior, tightness-looseness has consequences for everyday situations at home and in restaurants, classrooms, public parks, libraries, and the workplace: behavior that is deviant (like dressing different than others, talking out loud in libraries, arguing in public) is more accepted in loose than in tight cultures.[30] In sum, whereas imitation is part of all human cultures because it allows for social learning, the degree to which people value distinctiveness and deviance can differ depending on the culture.

CONCLUSION

Adults should know better than simply imitating other adults, shouldn't they? In this chapter, we learned that there are good reasons for doing so. And that we have basic psychological mechanisms which make it easier for us to do so. Imitation is a way of using heuristics to make quicker decisions in times when we have no time to think about a situation more elaborately. It provides adults with good-enough solutions. The fact that our brain is tuned on other people's faces and gazes helps us making these decisions. We use other people's gazes or expressions to make sense of complex or uncertain situations. Informational influence and normative influence play a key role in this. Particularly, people who look like us (belong to our group) are important sources of how to behave (what to imitate) or not to behave. We tend to follow other people (heuristics) in particular when we have less time or energy to carefully consider a situation. Based on the theory of social comparison, we have two options: comparing yourself to people who are more highly skilled than yourself to learn to do something better and comparing yourself to others who are less skilled to feel better about yourself. Research on imitation in adulthood in different contexts teaches us an important part about human motivation. For example, in regard to fashion, we like to imitate others because it gives us a feeling of social belonging. But we also at the same time like to distinguish ourselves from others to maintain our uniqueness. Imitating other people's behaviors can also tell us something about the social status of this person. The STEPPS model explains that there are six elements that make certain information catching resulting in imitation behavior: Social currency, Triggers, Emotions, Practical value, Public, and Stories. Examples throughout the chapter in the context of art, politics, crowd, and emergency situations illustrate that social learning, social comparison, and social norms explain our tendency to imitate others. Imitation allows for social learning. Across cultures there can be differences in how imitation is valued. In collectivistic cultures, the sharing of similarities with others is valued more than in individualistic cultures where individuals tend to emphasize their uniqueness. Also, in tight cultures, not imitating other people's behaviors (i.e., behaving defiantly) is less accepted than in loose cultures. Nevertheless, imitation is found in all cultures and nations across the world as it plays a key role in sharing customs and beliefs with other group members.

BOX 6.2 WHAT YOU SHOULD DEFINITELY REMEMBER FROM THIS CHAPTER

- In adulthood, imitation is important as it can give us quick answers on how to behave or not to behave in uncertain or complex situations. Other people help us make sense of these situations, and we therefore tend to imitate them. Imitation therefore allows for social learning.
- Social norms are an important part of imitation as they tell us what is usually done (descriptive norms) or what ought to be done (injunctive norms).
- We compare ourselves to others who are more skilled than us (upward comparison) to learn new skills and people who are less skilled than us (downward comparison) to make us feel better.
- Imitation occurs in different social contexts in adulthood such as fashion, hypes, art, politics, crowds, and emergency situations. Research among adults in these areas teaches us about the importance of imitation behavior and how imitation takes place or is valued.
- Imitation plays an important role in cultural development, and it helps people in a social group to share their customs and beliefs. However, across cultures, imitating others can be valued differently.

NOTES

1 Baumeister, R. F., & Leary, M. R. (1995). The Need to Belong: Desire for interpersonal attachments as a fundamental human motivation. *Psychological Bulletin, 117*(3), 497–529. https://doi.org/10.1037/0033-2909.117.3.497
2 Gigerenzer, G. (2008). Why heuristics work. *Perspectives on Psychological Science, 3*(1), 20–29. https://doi.org/10.1111/j.1745-6916.2008.00058.x

3 Langten, S. R. H., Watt, R. J., & Bruce, V. (2000). Do the eyes have it? Cues to the direction of social attention. *Trends in Cognitive Sciences*, *4*(2), 50–59. https://doi.org/10.1016/S1364-6613(99)01436-9
4 Young, A. W., Hellawell, D., & Hay, D. C. (1987). Configurational information in face perception. *Perception*, *42*(11), 1166–1178. https://doi.org/10.1068/p160747n
5 Gauthier, I. (2020). What we could learn about holistic face processing only from nonface objects. *Current Directions in Psychological Science*, *29*(4), 419–425. https://doi.org/10.1177/0963721420920620
6 Asch, S. E. (1956). Studies of independence and conformity: I. A minority of one against a unanimous majority. *Psychological Monographs: General and Applied*, *70*(9), 1–70. https://doi.org/10.1037/h0093718
7 McDonald, R. I., & Crandall, C. S. (2015). Social norms and social influence. *Current Opinion in Behavioral Sciences*, *3*, 147–151. https://doi.org/10.1016/j.cobeha.2015.04.006
8 Cialdini, R. B., Reno, R. R., & Kallgren, C. A. (1991). A focus theory of normative conduct.pdf. *Journal of Personality and Social Psychology*, *58*(6), 1015–1026. https://doi.org/10.1037/0022-3514.58.6.1015
9 Jacobson, R. P., Mortensen, C. R., & Cialdini, R. B. (2011). Bodies obliged and unbound: Differentiated response tendencies for injunctive and descriptive social norms. *Journal of Personality and Social Psychology*, *100*(3), 433–448. https://doi.org/10.1037/a0021470
10 https://www.hopperhq.com/instagram-rich-list//#FullTable
11 Festinger, L. (1954). A theory of social comparison processes. *Human Relations*, 7(2), 117–140.
12 Van der Zee, K. I., Buunk, B. P., De Ruiter, J. H., Tempelaar, R., Van Sonderen, E., & Sanderman, R. (1996). Social comparison and the subjective well-being of cancer patients. *Basic and Applied Social Psychology*, *18*, 453–468. https://doi.org/10.1207/s15324834basp1804_6
13 Owen-Crocker, G. R. (2011). Dress and identity. In *The Oxford Handbook of Anglo-Saxon Archaeology* (pp. 91–115). Oxford University Press.
14 Esposito, E. (2011). Originality through imitation: The rationality of fashion. *Organization Studies*, *32*(5), 603–613. https://doi.org/10.1177/0170840611405424
15 Berger, J. (2013). *Contagious: Why things catch on*. London: Simon & Schuster.
16 Niederkrotenthaler, T., Fu, K. W., Yip, P. S., Fong, D. Y., Stack, S., Cheng, Q., & Pirkis, J. (2012). Changes in suicide rates following media reports on celebrity suicide: A meta-analysis. *Journal of Epidemiological Community Health*, *66*(11), 1037–1042. https://doi.org/10.1136/jech-2011-200707

17 https://www.theguardian.com/film/2015/may/31/jaws-40-years-on-truly-great-lasting-classics-of-america-cinema
18 Newell, J., Salmon, C. T., & Chang, S. (2006). The hidden history of product placement. *Journal of Broadcasting & Electronic Media, 50*(4), 575–594. https://doi.org/10.1207/s15506878jobem5004_1
19 Nickerson, D. W. (2008). Is voting contagious? Evidence from two field experiments. *American Political Science Review, 102*(1), 49–57. https://doi.org/10.1017/S0003055408080039
20 Bhatti, Y., & Hansen, K. M. (2012). Leaving the nest and the social act of voting: Turnout among first-time voters. *Journal of Elections, Public Opinion & Parties, 22*(4), 380–406. https://doi.org/10.1080/17457289.2012.721375
21 Reicher, S. (2001). The psychology of Group Dynamics. In M. A. Hogg & R. S. Tindale (Eds.), *Blackwell handbook of social psychology: Group processes*. Boston, MA: Blackwell Publishers. Quotation from p. 182.
22 Reuters (2020). *Dutch PM tells citizens to relax, saying there's enough toilet paper for 10 years*. Reuters. Retrieved from: https://www.reuters.com
23 Littleproud, D. (2020). Don't panic, Australia. The coronavirus doesn't mean we'll run out of food. *The Guardian*, March 18. Retrieved from: https://www.theguardian.com/global/commentisfree/2020/mar/19/dont-panic-australia-the-coronavirus-doesnt-mean-well-run-out-of-food
24 Vaswani, K. (2020). Coronavirus: Why Singapore is so vulnerable to coronavirus spread. *BBC*, February 13. Retrieved from: https://www.bbc.com/news/world-asia-51480613
25 Drury, J. (2018). The role of social identity processes in mass emergency behaviour: An integrative review. *European Review of Social Psychology, 29*(1), 38–81. https://doi.org/10.1080/10463283.2018.1471948
26 Drury, J., Cocking, C., Reicher, S., Burton, A., Schofield, D., Hardwick, A., Graham, D., & Langston, P. (2009). Cooperation versus competition in a mass emergency evacuation: A new laboratory simulation and a new theoretical model. *Behavior Research Methods, 41*(3), 957–970. https://doi.org/10.3758/BRM.41.3.957
27 Swann, W. B., & Buhrmester, M. D. (2015). Identity fusion. *Current Directions in Psychological Science, 24*(1), 52–57. https://doi.org/10.1177/0963721414551363
28 Heyes, C. (2021). Imitation and culture: What gives? *Mind and Language*, 1–22. https://doi.org/10.1111/mila.12388

29 Kitayama, S., Mesquita, B., & Karasawa, M. (2006). Cultural affordancesand emotional experience: Socially engaging and disengaging emotionsin Japan and the United States. *Journal of Personality and Social Psychology*, *91*, 890–903. https://doi.org/10.1037/0022-3514.91.5.890

30 Gelfand, M. J., Raver, J. L., Nishii, L., 4, & Yamaguchi, S. (2011). Differences between tight and loose cultures: A 33-nation study. *Science*, *332*, 1100–1104. https://doi.org/10.1126/science.1197754

IMITATION IN LATE ADULTHOOD

INTRODUCTION

In our model presented in Chapter 1, we argue that uncertainty makes us prone to imitate other people. "If other people are doing this, it might be the right action". Generally speaking, when we get older and into late adulthood, we can see two inclinations. Some of us tend to become a little more uncertain about ourselves. We may start asking questions such as: What is my role in this world? Why is the world changing so fast? How can I keep up? If we feel that way, we may resort to imitation. Imitation can provide comfort. In contrast, other older people among us feel that we have seen the world and we know what's out there. We have the "been-there, done-that-attitude" and a strong sense of who we are. We know what we like and how we want to behave. Sometimes, we can express a quite extreme position: "At my age, I don't need anybody to tell me what to do!" We all know our stubborn parent or grand-parent, who thinks that, at their age, general norms and rules no longer apply to them. They feel free to express whatever comes to their minds. And they think they can do anything they like. Are these free spirits among us less likely to follow role models? Are they less likely to imitate? In this chapter, we will present evidence that older people are *more* likely to imitate others (see Figure 7.1), but on other occasions, they are *less* likely to imitate others. Hang on, what is going on here? Please bear with us and read on till the end of this chapter!

DOI: 10.4324/9781003175056-7

Figure 7.1 Chinese couple imitating each other by wearing the same shirt – and smile!
Source: shutterstock.com.

WHY AND WHEN DO OLDER PEOPLE IMITATE MORE?

As we become older, we can become uncertain in several ways. First, we may feel uncertain when we retire from work. This is a major life event![1]

We leave behind a workplace, often including colleagues. We leave behind an important connection with society. And we leave behind a sense of contribution to society. Thus, when we retire, we often feel uncertain and can be unhappy. The future is vague for us. We don't know for sure what's to come next. How can we make our lives meaningful again after retirement?

This is one reason why people have argued for a smoother transition between work life and retirement. For example, we can decide to work less hours each year we get nearer to our retirement age (this retirement age differs a lot between countries, by the way). Is that a good idea? Yes. We might experience less retirement stress if we prepare ourselves a little by working less when we're near the retirement age. We can start building up our "life after retirement" before we actually retire. This will result in a smoother transition between work life and retirement. For example, we might try and find volunteering work or spend more time playing table tennis with others. Such actions will have both physical and social benefits. We are healthier and happier when we do things together with others, in particular in groups.[2]

By the way, uncertainty is not only likely to happen for older people who retire but also present in young athletes who retire from sports.[3] A fascinating study looked at what happens when athletes retire from their sports career. They can experience lower life satisfaction, partly because it was unclear what their future lives would look like. And not knowing what your life will look like creates feelings of uncertainty obviously. And what do we do when we feel uncertain? If you've come this far in this book, you should know by now that we look for clues about how to behave and that we find these clues from other people. So, we start imitating them.

When we feel uncertain, we can read books with tips and tricks: "How to deal with … [please fill in your area of uncertainty, for example, a difficult colleague; a child that won't listen; the death of your mother; an empty nest, etc.]". Or we might search for such information on the internet and may join an online self-help group with like-minded people. Still others might go to a house of prayer to find answers to their questions. In sum, there are many ways in which we, when we face uncertainty, can find rules or norms about how to behave. Ever wondered why so many retired people start making a family tree? It's not just that now they have the time to do it, it also provides them with lots of good things: purpose, daily activity, and interaction with other family members. And it also provides them with a sense of identity and certainty: this is me in the bigger picture of the universe!

The second way older people can become uncertain is that they feel that their mental capacities and/or physical abilities are no longer top-notch. They may start forgetting things more often. They may experience that even a little exercise can be really tiring. These changes may make people feel a little more uncertain about themselves. This uncertainty can translate into imitation. Is there evidence for this?

Indeed, there is evidence for this tendency to imitate others among older people. Specifically, people diagnosed with dementia show less automatic imitation.[4] Dementia is often associated with uncertainty, as people experience a loss of control in their lives.

Imitation reduces uncertainty because it gives us the certainty that someone else has done the same.

So, when our partner orders a cappuccino, we order one too, as we are certain it is the right drink at this time of the day in this context (provided that your partner is not suffering from dementia as well). We might have liked a cold beer, but that might be a less appropriate drink to order at 9 am during a visit to your grandchild's school! You'd better be on the safe side and order that cappuccino.

So, among older people, food consumption might depend on imitation of others. When others are not around, imitation cannot take place. Consequently, older people might eat less.[5] Indeed, loneliness and social isolation are the important factors that make older people eat less. They might feel depressed due to a loss or a reduction of their social network. This can lead to a loss of their appetite.

Another interesting theme that emerges when we get older is our legacy. This includes fascinating questions such as: Where do I come from? What is my ancestry? But also: What have I achieved in my lifetime? What do I leave behind? Therefore, as indicated before, as older people, we *en masse* go out and make our family tree. Yes, that creates some order in our lives: "This is where I came from, these are my children, these are my grandchildren who will live on when I am gone."

We don't like to be reminded of the fact that we're mortal. In fact, this can cause quite some stress and anxiety in us.[6] But hey, if there is some way in which I can continue to live after my death, that would be a great relief! And thus we, as older people, start searching for clues and ideas. We may start drawing paintings all of a sudden. Or we may write poems.

Interestingly, when we are reminded of our own mortality, we support our culture more. We do this because we think that our culture will be around after our death and that new people from our culture will nurture and nourish our world view. So, this may lead older people to experience a shared sense of cultural world view.

Finally, a word on internalizing stereotypes. The stereotypes about older people tend to be about being less healthy, being less fit, and being slow and not energetic. For some people, this can become a *self-fulfilling prophecy*[7]: they might act in line with the

BOX 7.1 LET'S ALL IMITATE THE IMITATION GAME!

As argued in Chapter 1, imitation leads to liking. We like other people who are like us. Does that work for older people as well? Sure enough! In a nice study, a group of older people from Haifa (71–98 years old) did two tasks: a physical exercise task and an imitation task.[8] A subgroup of them first did the exercise task and then the imitation task. Another subgroup of them did the same tasks in reverse order. The order did not matter. What mattered was the imitation!

The researchers borrowed a method often used in theater. It consists of three parts of three minutes. In the first part, person A has to follow the body gestures or movements of person B for three minutes. In the second part, the roles are reversed: person B has to follow the body gestures or movements of person A for three minutes. In the third and final part, there is no explicit leader or follower. The pair is simply instructed to imitate each other's gestures and movements for three minutes. This means they have to watch carefully and follow each other's gestures and movements.

What happens? Well, first of all, people reported that the imitation task was a more positive experience than the exercise task. They also thought the other person was more responsive in the imitation task than during the exercise task. Interestingly, they performed better on several cognitive tasks after the imitation task than after the exercise task. Specifically, they scored higher on three tests measuring attention, concentration, and working memory. The bottom line is that when we get older, we all should imitate the imitation game!

stereotype because they might believe in that stereotype. This makes it look like older people imitate each other: they all walk slowly.

To conclude, older people may experience uncertainty about their social life and their mental and/or physical abilities. This uncertainty may translate into the motivation to imitate others, especially among people suffering from dementia. But hold on: that's not the whole story. It gets slightly more complex than this.

WHY AND WHEN DO OLDER PEOPLE IMITATE *LESS*?

Yes, indeed, older people may imitate more when they feel uncertain. But there are good reasons why not *all* older people increase their imitation. We give you a couple of reasons. First, you need to have the capacity to imitate. And when these capacities are reduced, imitation drops. In fact, researchers even developed a simple imitation task to detect early signs of dementia.[9] Having difficulties with imitation of finger gestures can be a sign of an early form of dementia.

The capacity argument is also in line with studies showing reduced imitation among patients with Alzheimer's disease. This is especially the case for patients who have passed the initial stages of the disease. And, in this case, it involves relatively complex movements. An example of such a movement is the two-hand movement task. In this task, individuals are asked to copy a movement where the hands do different tasks at the same time, for example, holding a jar with one hand while opening the lid with the other hand. A statistical analysis of all the studies about this topic confirms this pattern.[10]

BOX 7.2 ABOUT ALZHEIMER'S DISEASE AND DEMENTIA

Alzheimer's disease is the most common form of dementia. It is a progressive disease. So, it gets worse over time. It involves parts of the brain that control thought, memory, and language. It causes a decline in intellectual functioning.

Alzheimer's disease might begin with mild memory loss. "What was the name again of the village that we went to yesterday?" Subsequently, we might lose the ability to carry on a normal conversation. And we may respond in an uncertain manner to the environment. Ultimately, it can seriously undermine our ability to carry out daily activities and routines, including imitation.

In most studies, researchers test imitation by looking at arm movements. Are patients with Alzheimer's disease able to imitate simple and complex arm movements? Well, you might have guessed it: patients with Alzheimer's disease find that difficult! For example, one study showed that patients with Alzheimer's disease displayed less smooth and less continuous arm movements than a control group without Alzheimer's disease.

Interestingly, this is not only true for people with Alzheimer's disease. Generally, when we get older than 70, our (previously often automatic) imitation skills are reduced. This is true for all of us! It doesn't matter whether or not we suffer from Alzheimer's disease.

To make the picture even darker, here is the second reason we might imitate less when we get older: we tend to forget more things.[11] Everyone above 50 years knows this. This is most likely because our working memory decreases. Importantly, for our discussion, we tend to forget about social norms as well when we get older.[12] For example, when we get older, we know less well whether or not it is socially acceptable to "spit on the floor" or to "talk out loud during a film in a cinema." So next time you meet older people who talked loud during the movie and afterwards spat on the floor just outside the door of the cinema, please bear in mind: they can't help it, as it's not them, it's their age!

In addition, this drop in knowledge about how to behave (social norms) becomes more apparent when we suffer from dementia or a long-term psychiatric disorder.[13] With reduced knowledge of how one should behave, imitation behavior drops (see Chapter 6 for the role of social norms in imitation during adulthood).

Interestingly, we also become less fluent in reading other people's emotions when we get older. Remember the newborn babies in the hospital who all started crying after one baby started – the opening example in Chapter 1. Well, that is less likely to happen when we get older! This is because we are less able to recognize the emotions that are displayed by others when we get older.

BOX 7.3 DON'T PICK YOUR NOSE IN PUBLIC!

What is normal? That is a crucial question when you study social norms. For example, in one study, researchers devised 22 items about socially appropriate behavior and inappropriate behavior. For example, for the following behaviors, they asked to what extent people thought they were socially acceptable and appropriate (answering options were yes or no):

- Pick your nose in public (Don't even try. If you must, go to the toilet).
- Eat ribs with your fingers (That's fine).

- Eat pasta with your fingers (Nah, don't do it).
- Blow your nose in public (Not ideal, but it can be done).
- Cut in line if one is in a hurry (Just don't do it).
- Tell a coworker your age (That's fine! Please go ahead).

In this study, first 38 healthy people (45–87 years) who had lived more than 20 years in the US filled out the items. Subsequently, there was another group of 122 US citizens (ages 46–92 years) who filled out the same items. So, people can be ranked in terms of how much they know about social norms.

Interestingly, they made a distinction between two types of errors:

1. Breaking a social norm (e.g., picking your nose in public)
2. Over-adhering to a non-norm (such as indicating that it is not appropriate to eat ribs with one's fingers).

Needless to say, norms are culturally determined.[14] This means we cannot simply copy and paste the list of items that were devised by Kramer et al. and use it in another context. Although we do advise never ever pick your nose in public, not even on the Antarctic (Figure 7.2)!

Figure 7.2 Don't forget the social norm: Eating ribs with your fingers is allowed. For young and old people!

Source: shutterstock.com.

Second, and obviously, the type of the potentially imitated behavior matters. For example, when people get older, they imitate violent others less. Ever seen a violent gang of older people molesting youngsters? They are not that common! Indeed, younger people are more likely than older people to imitate aggressive behavior. For example, after being exposed to acts of terror in their social circle, young people are more inclined than older people to join that group. This is why scholars talk about "a bunch of guys" theory usually: young men who know each other form a group in which violent behavior gets imitated.[15] The same is true for copycat suicide: this is more likely to happen among younger adults than among older people.[16]

Third, it depends on culture, in particular how much certainty people experience.[17] For example, in the US and Sweden, people generally experience more certainty than in Romania. Interestingly, in high-certainty countries, older people feel more in control of their lives than younger people. And thus, older people are expected to imitate less than younger people. It is fascinating that this pattern is not visible in low-certainty countries. In such countries, there is no relation between age and feelings of control.

Another reason why older people might imitate *less* is because there are less role models available. The role models in the (traditional and social) media often are younger than they are. This makes it more difficult to find suitable role models for older people. This reduces their capacity to imitate. Clothing commercials, for example, often use young models. These younger role models do not give an answer to this urging question of a frustrating grandmother: "What shall I wear during my granddaughter's wedding?"

Finally, older people tend to have created habits. Habits that they like! And so, they may be less likely to follow the latest trends. For example, they may not want to wear the newest styles of clothing. They may not appreciate the hottest trends in popular music. They also may not always be that excited to go to new and faraway places for holidays – they might enjoy a favorite holiday destination that is closer just as much.

Thus, there is some evidence that as we get older, we imitate less. Part of the reason is that there are less role models present in the media when we get older. We may also have developed habits that we like and are not interested in the latest trends. In addition, we forget about social norms, in particular when dementia kicks in. Diminished imitation behavior is particularly true for complex movements and for violent behavior. No big deal. We just have to accept that when we get into our 70s, we may find it harder to imitate a serial killer. Our lack of imitation when we get older may also be due to the feeling of being more in control of our lives, at least in safe countries.

CONCLUSION

And what now? We have two camps here: both more and less imitation among the older people. Who is right? Luckily, there is a way to reconcile these contradictory findings. It looks like when we get older, we may be highly *motivated* to imitate others. But at the same time, especially after we reach 70, we forget the social norms and our physical *ability* to imitate seems to drop. This is especially true for more complicated physical movements (and for violent behavior). Thus, what should we do after we have reached 70? Avoid learning complicated new dances!

BOX 7.4 WHAT YOU SHOULD DEFINITELY REMEMBER FROM THIS CHAPTER

- As older people, we still want to imitate others.
- This is because we experience uncertainty.
- This is particularly true when we suffer from mild forms of dementia.
- But as we get older, we also forget about social norms.
- This is even stronger when we suffer from dementia.
- We find less role models to imitate.
- We have developed habits that we like.
- We may resort to act in line with the stereotype about older people.
- After we turn 70, our ability to imitate drops.

NOTES

1 Crosswell, A. D., Suresh, M., Puterman, E., Gruenewald, T. L., Lee, J., & Epel, E. S. (2020). Advancing research on psychosocial stress and aging with the Health and Retirement Study: Looking back to launch

the field forward. *The Journals of Gerontology, 75*(5), 970–980. https://doi.org/10.1093/geronb/gby106

2 Jetten, J., Branscombe, N. R., Haslam, S. A., Haslam, C., Cruwys, T., Jones, J. M., …, & Thai, A. (2015). Having a lot of a good thing: Multiple important group memberships as a source of self-esteem. *PLoS One, 10*(5) e0124609. https://doi.org/10.1371/journal.pone.0124609

3 Webb, W. M., Nasco, S. A., Riley, S., & Headrick, B. (1998). Athlete identity and reactions to retirement from sports. *Journal of Sport Behavior, 21*, 338–362. https://link.gale.com/apps/doc/A399107386/AONE?u=amst&sid=bookmark-AONE&xid=db39b586

4 Bisio A., Casteran, M., Ballay, Y., Manckoundia, P., Mourey, F., & Pozzo, T. (2016). Voluntary imitation in Alzheimer's disease patients. *Frontiers in Aging Neuroscience, 8.* https://doi.org/10.3389/fnagi.2016.00048

5 Donini, L., Savina, C., & Cannella, C. (2003). Eating habits and appetite control in the elderly: The anorexia of aging. *International Psychogeriatrics, 15*, 73–87. https://doi.org/10.1017/S1041610203008779

6 https://en.wikipedia.org/wiki/Terror_management_theory Or read the book: Solomon, S., Greenberg, J., & Pyszczynski, T. (2015). *The worm at the core: On the role of death in life.* Random House.

7 Bargh, J. A., Chen, M., & Burrows, L. (1996). Automaticity of social behavior: Direct effects of trait construct and stereotype activation on action. *Journal of Personality and Social Psychology, 71*, 230–244. https://doi.org/10.1037/0022-3514.71.2.230

8 Keisari, S., Feniger-Schaal, R., Palgi, Y., Golland, Y., Gesser-Edelsburg, A., & Ben-David, B. (2022). Synchrony in old age: Playing the mirror game improves cognitive performance. *Clinical Gerontologist, 45*, 312–326. https://doi.org/10.1080/07317115.2020.1799131

9 Nagahama, Y., Okina, T., & Suzuki, N. (2015). Impaired imitation of gestures in mild dementia: Comparison of dementia with Lewy bodies, Alzheimer's disease and vascular dementia. *Journal of Neurology, Neurosurgery & Psychiatry, 86*, 1248–1252. http://dx.doi.org/10.1136/jnnp-2014-309436

10 Krehbiel, L. M., Kang, N., & Cauraugh, J. H. (2017). Age-related differences in bimanual movements: A systematic review and meta-analysis. *Experimental Gerontology, 98*, 199–206. https://doi.org/10.1016/j.exger.2017.09.001

11 Morris, R. G., Gick, M. L., & Craik, F. I. M. (1988). Processing resources and age differences in working memory. *Memory and Cognition, 16*, 362–366. https://doi.org/10.3758/BF03197047

12 Van den Berg, E., Poos, J. M., Jiskoot, L. C., Montagne, B., Kessels, R. P. C., Franzen, S. et al. (2021). Impaired knowledge of social norms in

dementia and psychiatric disorders: Validation of the social norms questionnaire–Dutch version (SNQ-NL). *Assessment, 29*, 1–12. https://doi.org/10.1177/10731911211008234

13 Van den Berg et al. (2021). See above.

14 Shteynberg, G., Gelfand, M. J., & Kim, K. (2009). Peering into the "magnum mysterium" of culture: The explanatory power of descriptive norms. *Journal of Cross-Cultural Psychology, 40*, 46–69. https://doi.org/10.1177/0022022108326196

15 Sageman, M. (2004). *Understanding terror networks*. Philadelphia: University of Pennsylvania Press.

16 Rosario, A. L. C. (2019). Influencing suicide rates among the elderly. *Comparative Sociology, 18*, 757–790. https://doi.org/10.1163/15691330-12341513

17 Lawrie, S. I., Eom, K., Moza, D., Gavreliuc, A., & Kim, H. S. (2020). Cultural variability in the association between age and well-being: The role of uncertainty avoidance. *Psychological Science, 31*, 51–64. https://doi.org/10.1177/0956797619887348

8

CONCLUSION

WHAT HAVE WE LEARNED SO FAR?

In this book, we've discussed the many interesting ways we imitate others. In Chapter 1, we introduced the two routes of imitation: the learning route and the social route. In the learning route, we imitate others to solve a problem, for example, the tricky problem of "how to use the new printer at the office?". By copying one of our coworkers, we can probably get the job done more quickly than if we would try to solve it on our own. In the social route, we try to figure out how to behave, so we can feel happy about ourselves as members of social groups. For example, we look at what kind of clothes our coworkers are wearing in order to melt in with the crowd. Hence, if all of our coworkers wear fancy dresses and suits, we will copy them. We decide that our tennis shoes are never to be worn at the office. This way, our chances of our colleagues liking us are increased.

In Chapter 2, we defined imitation and differentiated it from similar forms of behavior, such as learning by instruction or complementary behaviors. (Remember a handshake is a complementary behavior, even though the two people shaking each other's hands are doing the exact same.) Next, various theories on imitation were discussed. Why do humans imitate, for example? We've learned that there are two reasons why humans imitate: to learn effectively and to gain approval by others – or, in other words, a learning route and a social route as described in Chapter 1. We've also learned that not all people are equally likely to be copied. We tend to imitate

DOI: 10.4324/9781003175056-8

experts over novices, people with a high status in society over people with a lower status, and those who look like us over people who we think are different from ourselves. Lastly, we learned about how our brains are programmed for imitation and that some brains might be more programmed to do so than others.

Starting from Chapter 3, we examined imitation across the life span. Specifically, in Chapter 3, we learned about imitation in infancy. The very youngest of humans appear to be already prone to imitate others: a six-week-old baby can already stick out his tongue when he sees an adult doing this. However, we've also learned that this is very much under debate. How do we know for sure this is imitation, and not mere stimulation? After all, we cannot ask these tiny humans why they show these behaviors. We've learned that psychologists favor the idea that imitation is learned because there is simply lack of evidence that imitation is innate. Sorry parents!

In Chapter 4, we learned about imitation in childhood. Young children like to imitate the adults they encounter in their everyday lives in play. This form of play is called *pretend play*, for example, when a six-year-old pretends to be daddy who is vacuuming the living room. Pretend play helps to develop creativity, language, and social skills. One especially important skill described in this chapter is called *theory of mind*, dubbed as the "mind reading skill". This skill is thought to be important for imitation. However, more research is needed to find the exact manner in which these two skills (mind reading and imitation) are related. In this chapter, we also learned about model learning. This is learning merely by observing someone else. Proof for this theory was famously demonstrated by the Bobo doll study: children who observe someone playing aggressively will also show aggressive behaviors themselves. Next, we learned that children are more likely to copy friendly strangers than strangers acting aloof. And, just like adults, children are also likely to imitate people who are similar to them (the *likeness bias* described in Chapter 2). Next, we learned that children learn language through imitation. Where adults need instruction and much practice to learn a new language, children learn instantly without much effort. Simply being exposed to the language is enough! Lastly, we learned how fear can be learned by observing others. When toddlers view their parent react fearfully to a rubber snake, they tend to be fearful of this harmless toy themselves too. However, when parents hold it together and act neutral, their youngsters are more likely to play with the toy.

Chapter 5 focused on imitation in adolescence. What do we know about teenagers? This period is very interesting from the viewpoint of imitation, as we learned that imitational behaviors peak in adolescence. We learned that adolescence is a time of "storm and stress". It is an age period in which we face uncertainty and ask ourselves the questions who we are and where we belong. The developmental psychologist Erik Erikson (1902–1994) coined this identity search as a challenge we face. In this period, we imitate others who are role models for us, such as influencers on social media which play a central role in many of contemporary adolescents' lives. Peers form a strong influence on our behaviors and set the norm. This may lead to positive behaviors, but also to risky behaviors. As we reviewed in Chapter 5, peers are a source of social support, but can also tempt us to engage in violence, smoking, alcohol use, risky driving, and substance use. We also saw that in this age period, extreme negative behaviors can occur under the influence of role models in the media. School shootings, copycat suicide behaviors, and engagement in criminal and terrorist groups are sad examples where imitation plays an important role. Nevertheless, if the challenge to develop a positive and strong identity is met, and we do develop a positive self-view and find our place in society, then this forms a solid basis for the next developmental stage: adulthood.

In Chapter 6, we looked at imitation in adulthood. This is one of the longer chapters for a good reason. First, this age group is the longest spanning from roughly 18-year-olds till about 50-year-olds (or 65-year-olds, opinions differ). There is simply more to cover. Second, most scientific studies are conducted with adult participants, as they are by far the easiest to include in studies. Adults can decide themselves to participate, as opposed to children who would need at least a parent's approval. Hence, a large age group that is easy to study results in many studies to cover! In this chapter, we learned that (even) adults are prone to imitate others, even when this seems very silly. In the famous study from Asch, we saw that adults copy the group consensus (asserting that a certain line is shorter than others, even though it is clearly not). We are prone to follow social norms. These norms can be either descriptive (what is *normal* behavior, such as waiting in line at the grocery store checkout) or injunctive (what most people *approve* of, or *disapprove* of, for example, wearing a mask during a pandemic). Under time crunch, we are more likely to follow descriptive norms. However, when we have time to think clearly, we are more likely to follow injunctive norms. Next, we learned that we could compare ourselves to people who we think are more successful (upward comparison) or those who are less successful (downward comparison). We are more likely to copy those who we think are more successful. Rings a bell? Rightfully so, we dubbed this the *prestige effect* in Chapter 2! Finally, this chapter described some examples where we tend to copy others. Hypes (like the ice bucket challenge in 2014) are a clear example of imitation spreading quickly. They run on six things: a social currency (e.g., looking good to your friends), a triggering event (e.g., a video), emotions (e.g., admiration, excitement), public (e.g., spreading through social media), practical value (e.g., spreading awareness for the illness amyotrophic lateral sclerosis [ALS]), and stories (e.g., teach others about ALS via a quick video).

Lastly, in Chapter 7, we looked at imitation among older people (65+ years). We learned that there are two opposing theories about imitation in this stage of life. The first holds that people in late adulthood imitate *more* because they experience more uncertainty. They might feel more uncertain about their decreasing mental and physical abilities, which, in turn, can motivate them to imitate others. For example, if your grandma has troubles remembering what is socially accepted to order during brunch, she might simply copy your order to be sure she got it right. The other theory holds that people in late adulthood imitate *less*. How many copycat crimes have you seen conducted by an older person? Additionally, there is some evidence that people with dementia show less imitation. Finally, role models for older people are often missing from (social) media: who do they have to imitate? The overall conclusion should be conservative though. People in late adulthood are very underrepresented in scientific studies. Thus, there is little scientific evidence on imitation in elderly people. With an increasing number of people who are in late adulthood (we do get older and older!), more research is certainly welcome!

HELICOPTER VIEW OVER THE AGES

We have chosen to divide the chapters chronologically, with each chapter describing interesting studies on imitation for a different age group. Now, we would like to take a helicopter view and look at the differences and similarities across these groups.

To start with a similarity: Across all ages, there are the two reasons *why* we might copy others. We imitate to learn and to fit in: the learning route and the social route of imitation. The learning route helps us learn new things etc. A young child copies their parent to learn how to drink out of a cup, a teenager might copy their classmates' homework to prevent hours of writing an essay themselves, and an older person copies their friends' cruise ship holiday to ensure having a good time without having to compare every possible holiday. The social route drives us to imitation to achieve closeness to others or to be liked by others at the very least. Thus, young infants imitate the melodical sounds when their caregiver sings a song, teenagers copy their peers to try and fit in the group, and adults willingly engage in trends like the ice bucket challenge so their friends on social media can think they are good people.

On a more in-depth level, *who* we are likely to imitate also seems to be the same across the ages. For example, the likeness bias is found to hold true in both children and adults. Both young children and adults are more likely to copy people who are similar to them. Thus, a four-year-old is more likely to copy another four-year-old over a teenager. And a hardcore Barcelona fan is more likely to copy a fan of the same soccer team over a Real Madrid fan. Also, the prestige bias seems to hold true for children, teens, and adults. The more status someone has – from popular kids in class to famous soccer players – the more likely they are to be imitated.

Lastly, we are more likely to imitate others when we feel uncertain. This feeling of uncertainty can manifest itself in many ways. Take, for example, a situation where there is little time to think. Let's suppose that you are in a foreign country, and you hear a loud siren go off. People around you are startled, and all seem to run in a particular direction. What's the best thing you can do? Follow them of course! Perhaps they know there is an emergency exit nearby or they know the protocol for natural disasters you do not. In case of doubt, follow the crowd. Uncertainty can also be a more prolonged state. Arguably, the most uncertain time of one's life is adolescence. For some, high school is a fun experience. For others, it is awfully complex. Everyone wants to fit in with the cool kids. But many find it difficult to navigate all the unspoken rules teenagers have. These rules seem to continuously change as well. The one moment you *have* to wear skinny jeans, the next those are terribly old-fashioned, and mom jeans are in fashion. Perhaps this is why teens are most prone to imitation: they experience a constant level of uncertainty on how to behave. And lastly, uncertainty can also be simply that you do not know something and are interested in learning. For example, a toddler would like to build a big tower. By watching their older siblings build this tower, they too can learn how to make one. Thus, through imitation, their uncertainty (how does one build a tower?) decreases.

Now, onto the differences. What do we know is typical for specific age groups? In Figure 8.1, we have drawn how the amount of imitation behavior develops with age. First, as described in Chapter 3, we know that there is no clear proof of actual imitation in newborn babies. With the lack of proof, scientists adopt the view that imitation is learned, not innate. Similarly, there are mixed findings regarding imitation in the latest seasons of life. Whilst some evidence suggests the elderly are *more* prone to imitation, other evidence suggests they imitate *less* often than adults. For both the youngest and the oldest of humans, we must conclude that simply more research is needed.

Second, we know that language learning is something left to the youngsters. You might have noticed this yourselves. Children can learn language without any deliberate effort. Parents do not sit down with their four-year-olds going over the grammar rules on how exactly to construct a correct sentence. If parents for some reason decide to move to a different country, where people speak a different language, typically the children pick up the new language the fastest. After a few months, they can communicate with their peers. The parents, on the other hand, might struggle for years to properly learn the language. In addition, and in contrast to children, parents are likely to never lose their accent. As described in more detail in Chapter 4, our brains are more prone to learning language in childhood.

A third and final interesting difference is relevant for teenagers. In adolescence, imitation for social reasons seems to peak. In this age group, we see *more* imitation than in any other age group. Well, at least in individualistic Western countries. Blending in with the crowd is especially important to adolescents, in comparison with children and adults. You might recognize this too. Children typically want to please the adults in their lives: their parents, their primary school teacher, or maybe their tennis coach. However, once they become angsty teenagers, most children couldn't care less about what their teachers think of them. They want to

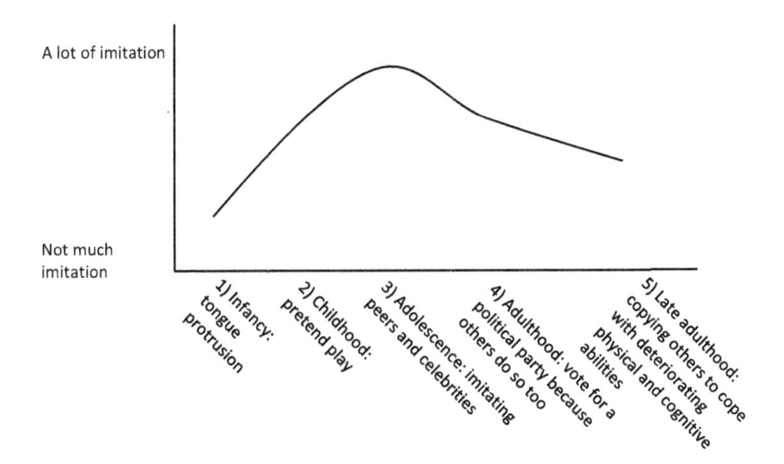

Figure 8.1 A figure showing the amount of imitation in each life stage with examples of behaviors. In adolescence, the amount of imitation behavior peaks.

impress their peers, wear the correct clothes, listen to the right music, and behave in a way they think their peers would approve. Hence, teens are more likely than any other age group to imitate their peers.

A CRITICAL LOOK AT US – THE AUTHORS

We, the authors of this book, have a confession to make. Maybe you already noticed this whilst reading the book. Maybe not. Regardless, we are sorry. In Chapter 2, we defined imitation. We claimed that imitation is behavior that is copied by one person, after observing someone else doing this very behavior. And we described this should be differentiated from complementary behaviors and synchrony. But did we consistently follow this definition? Were all studies included in this book focused on pure imitation? The short answer is no. But, before you get worked up and ask for a refund, please let us explain why!

We have tried our best to describe many interesting phenomena through the lens of imitation. However, real-world behavior is often complex and can be viewed with different lenses. Let's say, for example, you bought a bougie new salt dispenser. Your mother wants to use it and asks you how to operate this "machine". Simply shaking it did not have the desired effect. Thus, you explain to her to push the button and simultaneously twist (instructional learning), whilst also showing her how to do it with your hands at the same time (demonstration). Thereafter, your mother takes the salt dispenser and salts her food. At first glance, this is a good example of instructional learning. However, there is *also* an element of imitational learning, because your mother could have ignored what you said altogether, looked at what you did, and imitated your behaviors. Hence, some, if not most, real-world-behaviors fall in multiple categories – in this case imitation *and* instruction. "Pure imitation" is very difficult, and even impossible, to observe.

An example from our book would be the famous Asch study described in Chapter 6. Here, participants are asked to say which of two lines is longer than the other. There is a clear difference. Anyone who would be asked this alone would definitely pick line A (over line B) as the longer line. However, when asked this in a room full of people who all claim line B is longer (clearly the shorter line), many people will go with line B too. Typically, this experiment is used to show the power of social norms in groups. People don't like to stand out. Some might actually second guess themselves ("Maybe I am seeing it wrong?"), and others might not be convinced but don't want to stand out ("Line A is clearly correct, but I don't want them to think I am silly. I'll go along."). Either way, this study *also* tells us something about imitation: the effects of social norms by looking at imitational behaviors can be powerful. We've learned that people are likely to imitate others, if a group sets a norm.

A FINAL WORD

So where does that leave us? With a book full of imitation, you might think we're all one big imitating human family. Not quite so! Remember, in Chapter 2, we described the balancing act we all do: we imitate AND we stand out. That's because we have a need to belong (making us imitate others) AND a need to be unique (making us do other things than others).

Perhaps artists are a good example of people who have (developed) a strong need to be unique and different from other people. They often aim to create something that no one else has done before. This can be a new dance, a painting, a video installation, a song, a book, a movie, clothes, shoes, etc. Come to think of it: the list is endless.

Artists and art lovers are very keen to point this out to you. What makes the Mona Lisa art, but a printed copy of it, above your couch "fake", "ingenuine", or even "tacky"? Like so many art critics like to point out: art from IKEA is maybe decorative, but it's not art. If thousands of people have the same artwork … it's no longer art. Apparently, "true" art is unique. You might disagree or simply not care (rightfully so! If it makes you happy, keep those IKEA pieces in your house!). Nevertheless, critics agree that art needs to be unique. Copying others is generally frowned upon, or simply called *plagiarism*.

Thus, we are about to set on a different journey: a book not on imitation but on innovation! Full of rebels, people not playing by the rules, innovators, dissenters, visionary people, trendsetters, mavericks, reformers, prophets, revolutionaries, avant-gardists, modernizers, agitators, creative thinkers, insurgents, gurus, pioneers, imaginative leaders, protesters, discoverers, nonconformists, forerunners, inventors, renegades and developers! The world is full of them!

GLOSSARY OF TERMS

Biological development. The development of the brain (processes) in regard to behavior.

Cognitive skills. The ability to carry out mental processes such as solving problems, memorizing, anticipating future events, adaptation to new behaviors, learning, thinking abstractly, and making connections between different ideas.

Collectivistic culture. People in collectivistic cultures value interdependence more and tend to be other-centric.

Contagion effects. The phenomenon that acts carried out by an individual are copied by others who observe that behavior.

Culture. Shared customs and beliefs in a social group.

Descriptive norms. Norms that tell us something about what is usually done by other people who belong to our group.

Downward social comparison. It occurs when people compare themselves to others who are less skilled.

Emotion regulation. The ability to manage your emotions and to engage adaptively within your social environment.

Emotional development. The ability to anticipate our own and other's feelings.

False belief task. A task often used in psychological tests to assess a child's *theory of mind*. It assesses if children know that people act on their (false) beliefs, not on reality. The Sally-Anne task is a false belief task.

Heuristics. Rules of thumb that help us navigate the complex social world we are living in.

Hype. A feeling of expectation and desire for a particular thing to happen.

Identity fusion. A form of alignment with groups in which members experience a sense of oneness with the group.

Individualistic culture. People in individualistic cultures value independence and uniqueness of the individual more and tend to be ego-centric.

Informational influence. The phenomenon that people use other people's behavior to make sense of complex or uncertain situations.

Injunctive norms. Norms that tell us something about what most people approve or disapprove, or what *ought* to be done.

Loose culture. "Loose" cultures tend to have weak norms about how to behave and people in these cultures tend to be more tolerant of deviant behavior.

Mimicry. Imitation without the imitator being aware of it. Also referred to as *automatic imitation*. An example is copying someone's mannerism without intending to do so.

Mirror neurons. Nerve cells in the brain that are associated with imitation. These cells are active when merely observing others doing different behaviors, as if you were doing them yourselves too.

Normative influence. The tendency to follow the behavior of other members of our social groups.

Optimal distinctiveness theory. A theory that postulates that people have two needs that balance each other out: to belong and to be unique.

Ostracism. Exclusion from a society or group.

Overimitation. When someone imitates unnecessary behaviors in addition to the behaviors necessary to complete a task.

Pretend play. A form of play where acting as-if is central. The behaviors in play are not meant to reflect reality. Examples range from pretending to be a superhero, to playing house, and to pretending a banana is a telephone.

Product placement. A practice in which manufacturers of goods or providers of a service gain exposure of their products by paying for them to be featured in films and television programs.

Risky behaviors. Those behaviors that are not accepted in a society and can be harmful to the person or the environment.

Self-fulfilling prophecy. The phenomenon whereby a person's or a group's expectation for the behavior of another person or group serves actually to bring about the prophesied or expected behavior.

Social comparison. The process of comparing yourself to other people in terms of skills and behaviors.

Social development. Social and cultural environment in which an individual grows up.

Social learning. The process of learning customs and beliefs from other members of your social group.

Social learning theory. Learning new behaviors or skills merely by observing others (models). This form of learning was first described by the American psychologist Albert Bandura. This form of learning is also known as *model learning*.

Social norms. Beliefs or behaviors that a group of people accept as normal.

Theory of mind. A skill that children typically develop around the age of 4. Often named the "mind reading skill"; children learn that others can think, feel, or see differently than them.

Tight culture. "Tight" cultures typically have strong norms about how to behave, and there is a low tolerance for deviant behavior.

Upward social comparison. It occurs when people compare themselves with others who are more skilled on a particular task or behavior than they are.

Zone of proximal development (ZPD). An idea postulated by the Russian psychologist Lev Vygotsky. The ZPD is the difference between what a child can do by itself and what the child can do under the guidance of an adult or more capable peers. Vygotsky thought that children learn new skills best if they fall in the ZPD.

INDEX

Printed in the United States
by Baker & Taylor Publisher Services